BIG IDEAS FOR SMALL RETAILERS

John Castell

Oooo1745 ✓

First published in 2006 by Management Books 2000 Ltd
Forge House, Limes Road
Kemble, Cirencester
Gloucestershire, GL7 6AD, UK
Tel: 0044 (0) 1285 771441
Fax: 0044 (0) 1285 771055
E-mail: info@mb2000.com
Web: www.mb2000.com

Printed and bound in Great Britain by 4edge Ltd of Hockley, Essex

British Library Cataloguing in Publication Data is available

ISBN 1-85252-507-X

BIG IDEAS FOR SMALL RETAILERS

For a complete list of Management Books 2000 titles,
visit our web-site on http://www.mb2000.com

Preface

Prior to becoming a retailer, I was fortunate enough to hold several senior posts within a top-five UK Building Society and also an international banking group. Since leaving the world of financial services, I have become a seasoned High Street shopkeeper, which has been interesting to say the least. My experiences made me realise that everyday, somewhere, somebody just like you would also be starting, or wishing to improve their own small business. The aim of this book is intended to spare you some of the pain and frustration that I encountered early on, and to give some inspiration by way of well-tried initiatives.

Apart from divulging ways of improving your small enterprise, my experience gained from working with leading high street banks also enables me to offer a unique insight into retail finance-related subjects. Not advice on 'what is an overdraft, why do I need one and how do I get one' – this information is commonly available – but an explanation of the decision process which so often angers, frustrates and confuses retailers in general.

I will also reveal how small and medium sized retailers can obtain and offer 'own brand' store credit cards, so often perceived as the preserve of the multi-national chain stores, and even look at the possibility of creating own-brand products.

After trading successfully now for over a decade as an independent retailer, I thought it appropriate to also share information in respect of 'trade secrets', which are essentially a number of tricks and tips designed to win business away from competitors. This list isn't exhaustive, and you should be looking to add to it over time.

Embracing change is paramount to the success of small independent retailers. Whether you are embarking on your first retail ventures, or indeed are an established firm, you will need to continually plan for change, and indeed, expect change. Never allow yourself to become complacent. A diet of new ideas, new initiatives (many copied) and constant analysis are essential ingredients for success. This book encourages positive change and challenges traditional formats that small retailers tend to adopt. I would expect you to learn from other people's errors and, in the process, avoid making the same costly mistakes. You will also learn to fast track your business and ensure from the outset, to enjoy a high degree of credibility.

Common sources of 'self-help' tend to be polarised. That is, your Bank Manager will offer guidance on issues related to borrowing (and all the obligatory insurance and pension products which seem to accompany any visit to a bank these days); your accountant will advise on how to set up a set of accounting books (and probably introduce his friend the financial adviser who will gladly help you invest your profits 'for a fee'!). Your shop-fitter will tell you what he thinks will look good on the floor of your premises (because he's just done his kitchen with it at home). But, in my experience, no single individual will offer you concise and encompassing proven initiatives that are tailored to the needs of small retailers. Many of my opinions expressed will no doubt be viewed as cynical, and okay, disagree, but be warned that retailing, from the 'outside looking in' is not always what it appears to be. Motivation, ambition and greed by both suppliers and customers alike can make life challenging.

Clearly, from this we can see that professional advisers overlook much because they, individually, tend to be good at one thing. When my wife and I first ventured into retailing, we were not particularly good at any one thing (relative to retailing). We had an idea of what we wanted to do but everything we did was learnt the hard way.

You too, as an entrepreneur, however experienced, must develop a strong desire to learn many disciplines including the boring stuff: marketing, book-keeping, employment law, planning regulations, Information Technology and so on – or at least learn to delegate these tasks.

Whilst a high degree of understanding is required on the rules and regulations needed for day-to-day trading, learn to develop your sales techniques and associated skills. It will soon become apparent that time in business is very precious. Having to juggle the demands of the business with those of family life is also a necessary discipline, and requires the ability to stand back every once in a while and view circumstances objectively.

Finally, character and appeal need to be infused into your retailing project. But remember – the business of retailing has been around for many centuries. Most things have been done before – don't try to re-invent the wheel. Stick to the rules; create an edge over your competition, and above all else – be patient!

John Castell
January 2006

Dedication

Since opening a business in 1994 I have been privileged to be around some very special people to whom I will always remain indebted:

My wife Lynda – for always being there as a source of support, inspiration and affection. She also serves as a reminder that the best things in life are not always free.

My son James for being a valued occasional employee, and whose ability to become fired by me on a weekly basis, gives support to the theory that blood is thicker than water.

My daughter Becky – for encouraging me to become even more determined to 'do better' three times yearly, by handing me a bill for school fees at the end of each term.

And finally, to my manager Peter Richardson whose level of loyalty and commitment is only surpassed by his appetite for donuts, chocolate cookies and bad taste in music.

Contents

Introduction

The advice and methods contained within this guide are based on my personal experience of running a small business successfully for more than a decade.

'Big ideas for small retailers' was written with you in mind, simply because many years ago, I was in the position that you are in now. Whether you have just opened your business, or have been trading for some time, at some point you will be asking yourself – is this it? Is there nothing more I can do to help the business along? I've leased the premises, painted the walls and stocked the shelves. Advertised and ran promotions. But, where are the extra customers? The customers that make the difference between struggling to pay the bills and conversely enjoying the success of owning a thriving concern are hard won.

The truth is, in order to get those customers and keep them coming, you will have to develop a 'best practice'. This 'best practice' will encompass a strategy that goes beyond what you have already done. Your choice for taking your business forward doesn't have to be radical; but informed. In essence: evolution, not revolution.

If you have bothered to do much in the way of generic research before opening your business, you will have noticed that certain types of information are missing. Available information for small businesses tends to focus on market research, cash flow, profit and loss accounting, and income forecast. Essential reading, but not conducive to success when viewed in isolation.

Despite what you know, and what you are about to learn, it is always wise to remember that when retailing is brought down to the lowest common denominator it is simply about selling goods, and the following phrase should always be at the back of your mind – buy low – sell high. Whether you are selling dog biscuits or designer labels, this formula is the one to work with. Always aim to buy stock at the lowest possible price and aim to sell at the highest possible margin. Sounds ridiculously simple, but many experienced retailers lose sight of this when distracted by the million and one other chores needed to keep the business going: recruiting staff, dealing with Tax and VAT, book-keeping, maintenance of premises, preparing promotions, marketing plans and of course buying stock to fill the shelves.

My promise to you is that money will be saved and therefore profits will be increased by utilising just one of the many individual tips offered in the following pages.

Read on.

1

Image

It has often been said that the secret of becoming a successful small business is to pretend that the business itself it is really a big one; or at least part of a larger organisation. The image, which you create for your business therefore, in part, should mirror practices found in the larger successful chain stores. Lack of clutter, professional signage and the right ambiance are just a few of the main ingredients. A more detailed examination will soon follow but first let's start with the position of the retail premises. Residential estate agents will always state that the three most important things to remember when buying property are location, location and location. This is equally true when either buying or leasing your store premises, and if you are to create a 'winning' image, this advice should be taken on board at the outset.

When dealing with image, position is a key factor. There is little point in setting up shop as an upmarket retailer if your premises are situated in a deprived area of a large town or city. Sounds obvious, but look closely at stores that have recently closed down and question whether or not you would have opened that business in those premises, in that part of town. The previous tenants clearly thought that it was good enough for them! No one sets out to deliberately fail, but statistically, the majority of new businesses fail, and position, or lack of it, is a major contributing factor.

As the position of your premises is critically important for the success of your business, let's deviate from image for a moment to a piece of potential money saving advice. It was common practice in the recession of the early nineties for commercial landlords to offer rent-free initial periods. Three months were taken for granted with 12 months not being unusual, especially if the in-going tenant had plans to upgrade the premises. Contrary to popular belief, these initial rent free periods can still be attainable, and are therefore worth chasing, and if the premises have been vacant for a while, insist on at least three months rent free.

Quite often, budding retailers are so keen to get their ideas into practice they lose sight of the importance of position and in desperation, possibly through lack of choice, jump into the first premises that happen to come along. Be patient. As a sobering reminder of what could happen by taking a chance on your second choice of location, simply look back to the previous tenant. Did they move onwards and upwards or have they disappeared?

As an ambitious retailer, and not an aspiring geek, this next bit of information will look incredibly boring, and the temptation to ignore it will be great. However, this is probably one of the most important tips on how to ensure a degree of future sanity if all should go pear shape, and the need to exit from being self-employed becomes a forced issue. In simple terms, if your business goes down the pan, a safe escape route is needed, and one does exist.

Tip:

When agreeing terms of lease, your legal advisor will normally recommend that you insist on a break clause within the lease, allowing you to 'walk away' from the premises and the usual ongoing legal obligations of a standard lease which could include insurance, repairs and maintenance. This break-clause is normally restricted to just the first year or two. It allows you, the new trader, the opportunity to test your retailing concept, and conversely, allows the landlord to test the integrity of the new tenants - i.e. will you make a living, and will the landlord get his rent.

If you should fail within the agreed break-clause term, or believe that you won't survive for much longer, you can serve notice, via your solicitor, to exercise your right to quit, walk-away, and have no further liability to the landlord. Of course, the premises must be left in a good state of repair, and all utility bills remain your responsibility. But essentially, you are off the hook.

Conversely, should you not agree to a break clause before signing the lease, and cease trading, you will still be responsible for paying the rent, insurance, maintenance and so on and even paying an estate agent/business agent fees to introduce a willing tenant which is also acceptable to the landlord! These fast become the horror story situations where homes have to be sold in order to avoid repossession by creditor's claims.

You would think that everybody entering into a lease, especially for the first time, would be advised to negotiate a break clause by his or her legal advisers. Sadly, this is not the case. I don't pretend to know why. I could hypothesise and suggest that in some small towns, landlords and solicitors benefit equally from a regular turnover of tenants, as both normally end up financial winners. Landlords receive the benefit of newly renovated premises, which in turn means potential higher rent from the next in-going tenant, and lawyers receive their pound of flesh for dealing with the associated paperwork. However, this is wild speculation on my part, and of course couldn't possibly contain any element of truth! However, I do know, for a fact, that many retailers still enter into lease agreements without any knowledge of the break clause factor. If you have already committed yourself to a lease without a break clause, you may have no choice but to insist on one when you move to new premises.

Anyway, now that the 'legal' detour is out of the way, let's move on, and get back to 'image'.

Image

In the early years of trading within your store, there should be on-going experimentation – colour schemes, counter positioning, stock positioning and so on. This continual refinement is a necessary process and one which will ultimately allow your store to have the desirable established feel. This is subjective, but your aim is to make everything in the store gel. Everything has its place and only this long-winded process of experimentation will help you to achieve it. What you are doing in essence is formatting the store. This end format, if successful, will become your blueprint (unique identity) that will one day allow you to expand your empire.

Before going into further detail, I believe that whilst on the subject of image, staff and management have to be part of the plan. It is very difficult in these days of political correctness to advertise for the 'right' people, and yet image, in part, is as much to do with personal appearance as the shop-fit of the store. It is paramount that even the owner of a retail outlet must himself/herself be sensitive to the fact that their own 'image' may not be in keeping with the desired image of the business. I found myself in this very position and almost made myself redundant in the process.

Having developed a successful fashion business over a period of 10 years aimed at the 16 to 25 age group, I eventually became 'to old' to stand behind the counter. This is, of course, highly subjective, but relevant. In the same way that people would be sceptical about seeking help for a serious medical condition from a doctor that looks about 19 years old, or, wondering if, on the flight to Miami, the pilot that walked past you down the aisle, who looks like he was probably flying bi-planes in the first world war, will really make the journey. Is this about image or about being ageist?

Seriously though, think about it. Then think about how you fit into your business, and your target customers' perceptions. Another way to look at this factor, which I believe is also closely linked to credibility, is by asking yourself: Do I look authentic? In the same way that you would hesitate buying a Chinese or Indian takeaway, if the all the staff and cooks were white and English, your own customers could be put off by your own appearance, and for no other reason than lack of authenticity. This is of course an emotive issue as, in the above example, white English chefs could, in all probability, create Asian and Oriental dishes just as well. However, the customer will not always see it this way, because, to them, it lacks authenticity.

Whether situated on the High Street or stuck in a secondary position, this pretence of trading and belonging to something bigger and better is always desirable and possible. There are many tips in the following chapters to assist in creating the illusion of being part of a larger organisation. However, before creating, on paper, what will become your 'image' you first need to really understand your market – primarily, your customer profile and the competition faced. Questions such as: what do you consider to be your unique selling point, why do you feel you can do it better, or differently, than existing retailers and when should you start, are all questions that need answering.

Brands

I could have placed this paragraph under the 'buying section' but as the stock carried in any store is in itself fundamental in creating and sustaining the desired image, then combining this specific information with image is highly relevant.

When conducting your research, do more than the obvious. For example, if you decide to stock a particular clothing brand which is targeted at the under 25s, don't just check out boutiques in the immediate locality. Check local department stores, sports shops, including niche stores like bike shops, sunglass stores and even market stalls. Even catalogue stores such as Argos and Index (Littlewoods) in the UK, may be carrying the labels, which you aspire to sell exclusively to your customer base.

Retailing has changed vastly in recent years. Hard pressed superstore managers unable to achieve sales targets by conventional means have now become parasitic on niche markets and any alternative means of generating additional income for their stores is viewed as an opportunity to be tried. Supermarkets now sell medicine, cosmetics, TVs, loans, wetsuits, insurance, holidays and even cars (some even still sell food).

Before committing yourself to any brand, make sure that you know what you are buying into. Many sales reps will plead ignorance when confronted with questions of distribution of their company's products, stating that they only cover independent stores. They refer to national sales managers in a very vague way, almost to infer that they are irrelevant. Beware! They are lying to protect self-interests. Always be wary when agreeing to be supplied in your area exclusively with a specific product in this situation. Ask for further details of national sales/group arrangements before committing yourself to purchase. Later on, I will advise how to deal with the issue of 'broken promises' where companies have reneged on their agreements and have supplied your competitors with the same branded goods.

What is image?

In this chapter however, we are discussing image. A dictionary interpretation would be 'a representation of a likeness of a person or thing'. So what! You may ask. What the hell has this got to do with my store? Everything! I am always amazed to see new businesses open and then have to close soon after because they have failed to understand, and give themselves, the correct image.

Go back for a moment to the dictionary interpretation. Two key words stand out: **representation** and **likeness**. Your image has to reflect your chosen market. The image, which you create in your store, has to represent your customer profile, which in turn displays all of the characteristics associated with their 'likeness'. Consider the following extreme examples: would young skaters (under 14) consider going to Wal-Mart (supermarket) to buy skate clothing. Conversely, would sophisticated over 50s browse for T-shirts in a Skate shop which is packed with teenagers and belting out heavy metal music in the background? The answer to both scenarios is actually yes, but not in the desired way. Young mothers will drag their kids into Wal-Mart in the vain hope of meeting their kids' needs at minimal cost, and the over 50s would probably brave being shoved around a skate shop, despite the heavy metal music, in order to buy what their grandchildren really want for Christmas.

It appears then, that quite often, retailers are not synchronised with their chosen market, through no good reason other than their own age. Take the following example: a retailer, aged 45, may have identified an opportunity to sell fashionable products aimed at the under 20s. He sets up shop with all the right fitments, manages to obtain all the right fashion labels, and then decides to create a bit of atmosphere in the store by playing... mellow classical music! And this is where failure starts. Because of personal prejudice against 'in' music, he indulges himself with music he personally likes to the detriment of the business. Amazingly, this is not wild speculation about what could happen. I have encountered this scenario many times, and the result is always the same – lack of credibility, reduced sales or failure. Remember the old cliché – first impressions do count – and you do only get one opportunity to create a first impression.

Local needs

Always attempt to align your business to local needs and expectations. If you have difficulty doing this, get help. Ask friends and family for their views and act on them. Make sure that you also impress upon them the value of objective criticism. Don't bully them into saying what you want to hear. Your local Business Link – a free advisory service – may also be able to provide up-to-date market research on either the area from which you all ready trade or new territory where you wish to trade.

'Arty' people are always worth consulting. These people are usually involved in graphic design, photography and sign making, and if they can demonstrate success, consult them, even if you believe to have personally crafted the perfect image criteria.

Creative people are highly intuitive and have a keenly developed eye for what will work and what won't. At best, they will give you free valuable feedback on your proposal.

Credibility

Ultimately, your target is to create the correct image, one that offers instant credibility. Corporate identity is what you should be aiming for, as this offers excellent credibility, especially for new start-ups. You will know when you have achieved this because customers; especially visitors from other areas of the town or even other areas of the country, will ask if you have a branch near them. The size of your premises doesn't restrict you when trying to achieve this. Look at franchised outlets such as Tie Rack. Many of these trade in shops measuring less than 150 sq ft.

Your store's credibility is extremely important because customers spending large sums of money, possibly on a regular basis, want to believe, even on a subliminal level, that if they have a problem with a purchase, they can return it and get the problem resolved. Image and credibility therefore, are inextricably linked. It follows that imitating a chain store goes some way to instilling confidence in your chosen market, offering illusory but effective instant credibility.

This however, is not enough. Your store image must reflect the needs and aspirations of your customer base, and as such, it must be honed and fine-tuned to meet these customer expectations. To further demonstrate this, I offer the following examples of differing needs of customers, and I will draw an analogy with the hotel grading system.

A budget hotel room performs the same function as a five-star hotel room. It offers a bed to sleep on and a sink/bathroom, which allows you to wash. Prospective customers can choose this 'room' in either an un-graded or 2, 3, 4 or 5-star establishments. The main difference as far as the customer is concerned is the quality of the furnishings and the level of service offered. Gymnasiums, swimming pools, jacuzzis and so on are more often than not unused distractions that help the hotel to get the customer to part with more money than they need to. Point being – presenting the same product, in an elevated way, can allow you to trade at a higher level, and you will also realise with this analogy that people buy into what you are, and not just what you stock.

Achieving a corporate identity whilst being a combination of many factors is not dissimilar to the above hotel analogy. By building in certain (distractions) fitments and fittings, the 'established' look can be created. And whilst there may be a feeling of unwarranted expenditure, this is the only way to capture the essence of belonging to something bigger and better. Floor to ceiling panelling, suspended ceilings with dozens of eye-ball spotlights, quality floor coverings; such as Amtico and air-conditioning vents don't come cheap but are very effective when it comes to winning customers that prefer and expect this standard which is the corporate way.

Looking good is not always a recipe for success, but, professional looking displays and point of sale (often free from suppliers) combined with good presentation, i.e. uncluttered counter with a typed returns policy clearly displayed, placed ideally behind Perspex, and a PC-based EPOS system, will work wonders. Also, avoid putting posters and cards of any description in your window. The visiting Chinese circus may be good but it won't add any kudos to your business and at best is a distraction from what potential customers should be looking at – your stock!

Competition

Take a good look at what you consider to be the competition. Take note of their appearance, i.e. shop front, window display, point of sale and general store layout. Then take the trouble to find similar stores in other towns or cities. Finally, compile a list of all the good points and try to present yourself using these combined concepts. Large store chains spend many thousands of pounds on specialist design services; often involving top retail psychologists. They are not to be ignored. Many store layout profiles are based on a long history of experience. Everything is done for a reason.

Have you ever wondered why most large stores and supermarkets have their checkouts situated on the left of the entrance? Apparently, according to retail psychologist, most shoppers feel comfortable entering a store and walking to the right to start their browsing. This path continues around the store until, finally, they come to the checkout! If you are already trading and your counter is situated on the right when entering the store – it may be time for a change around. If you don't you are immediately confusing the customer; at a subliminal level, and may be losing sales. More on this aspect later.

Atmosphere?

This is often overlooked. Clearly, it would not be appropriate for all retailers to have wide screen plasma TVs mounted on their store walls, and the latest head-banging dance track belting out of ceiling mounted speakers. But done properly and aligned to your customer base, this can give your store an edge over the competition. Indeed the future of retail window displays is forecast to become a multi-media extravaganza. Traditional mannequins sporting the latest fashion or tiered shelving for general merchandise stacked pyramid fashion are about to be replaced by high tech imagery.

Multi-linked large flat screen plasma screens seamlessly combined to cover an entire shop front or internal wall will soon be displaying all kinds of products in a more dynamic, eye-catching way. This is the future – and this will happen. Ignore it at your peril. One final consideration on technology is the recently affordable projector. When connected to a PC running presentation software, a very professional in-store promotion can take effect, with or without music. This projected image can be used either in store window displays or beamed discreetly from the ceiling onto any flat, ideally white, surface inside on the store walls. Inter-space your labelled goods images with your own business adverts. This can take the form of bullet points, which highlight 'Today's special offer' to more powerful TV-style images. Projector-based, non-stop presentations when used in connection with software such as MS PowerPoint are only restricted by your imagination.

Music is also a very powerful ally, but due to the importance, and the question of whether or not you choose to play music in-store, I have devoted space on this issue to a chapter which looks at the pros and cons of doing so.

It's in the air

Did somebody mention smell! Coffee shops and bakeries have known for years that the aroma of their products pulls in customers. Why can't you choose a smell for your own store! City-based surf shops (many miles from the sea) are known to spray essence of coconut around to mentally stimulate the customer into believing that they are on holiday. How? The smell of coconut conjures up images associated with sun tan oil and the beach, immediately putting the brain into holiday mode and helping the customer to relax. Make them relax, feel comfortable and yes they *will* spend. Outdoor pursuit shops have also been known to spray pine scent but caution should be exercised as this can also smell like toilet cleaner! Cinnamon is usually a welcome smell around the festive season and, once again, sets the mood for shopping. Pump action sprays can be found in a variety of stores including car accessories shops and are very cheap.

Like everything else in life, moderation must be exercised. It's one thing to have a faint pleasant aroma to stimulate the senses, but overdoing it can make customers with a sensitive nose run out of the store muttering: 'What the #@!* is that awful smell?'

Managers of American shopping malls have been known to inject the air-conditioning with essence of strawberry and other flavoured aromas. This mass fumigation can have the opposite effect and can actually do more harm than good. In Europe, new legislation is finding its way into everything. Beware of being sued by staff and customers for having to inhale essence of anything!

Image detail

Attention to detail is one of the key attributes of a successful store. For example, if you are a fashion store, do all the hangers match in style and colour and do the heads all face the same way. This may sound very basic but you would be surprised by the number of stores which fail in the fundamentals. However, note the comments in the chapter dedicated to store security before adopting this practice – you may be surprised to learn that this neat system can be very useful for shoplifters!

Are pricing labels presented in a uniform way, typed (not hand marked) in the same colour and font? Paradoxically, stores catering for the bottom end of the market may wish to use fluorescent green/orange poster papers and large tip marker-pen. This look is the complete opposite of the aforementioned and serves to generate the 'closing down – everything is a bargain' look. However, use this type of price marking cautiously, as there is a fine line between generating extra foot traffic and sales, and suggesting that you really are closing down.

One of the many benefits of adopting a smart corporate image is that product pricing is generally accepted as non-negotiable. EPOS systems which are mentioned later also contribute to **not** making reductions at the counter – just because the customer has asked for it

Finally, image is just as important as the stock you carry. I have previously mentioned that people generally buy into what you stand for, just as much as what you sell, and to make this concept clearer, let's briefly look at how the fast food industry manages to fool people by utilising image as their core strength. International fast food chains are masters at using 'image' as a way of conveying standards and expectations. Food purchased from these food chains hardly ever wins awards for either the quality or content of the product they sell, and yet, due to clever systems, marketing and prominent, well-fitted units, people pour in day after day. Image, it seems, is everything.

2

Finance

Finance: is derived from the Old French word, finer, *and means to settle by payment.*

In retailing, finance covers a large spectrum of issues ranging from how you, the retailer, make and receive your payments, to both creditors and debtors, and how your customers make their payments to you. Amongst other things it can also relate to borrowings, loans, and overdrafts, and in the context of keeping these topics relevant, I intend to highlight some of the key areas, which lend themselves to perhaps be viewed from a different perspective.

Generating income from your customers is always a happy affair, paying suppliers isn't. One of your primary objectives is to realise payments taken from customers at the earliest opportunity and to delay payments to suppliers. Doing this efficiently takes effort, and requires an understanding of the processes that can be obstructive.

Governments around the world have passed various legal acts over the years to assist the suppliers of goods by allowing them to charge interest on outstanding debts. There is an irony about this as most government bodies have been proven to be the worst at paying bills. However, this form of remedy does have its shortcomings for the following reasons: in an ideal world, suppliers would like pre-payment for all goods despatched, and retailers would prefer to pay when all delivered goods have been sold. What tends to happen is that new traders have to pre-pay for goods before they are delivered, and after a period of time, say six months, more flexible terms are agreed, such as full payment within 30 days. For many retailers, these 30 days of grace, becomes the norm, and only if cash flow is tight do these terms start to stretch. This may temporarily help the trader but conversely, it puts the supplier on alert.

There is an alternative to the options above, which allows the retailer to have terms of payment extended to as much as 120 days! It doesn't cost a penny extra, and the goodwill between supplier and retailer is left intact. This alternative is called a payment plan, and will be discussed in greater detail later.

For the moment though, let's look at one key area that affects all sophisticated retailers – **profitability**.

Smart retailers are always looking for ways to improve business profits. Higher margins on sales, decreasing expenditure, smarter sales techniques, joint ventures with suppliers, more efficient use of the internet – the list goes on and on.

'Turnover is vanity – profits are sanity' is a well-known saying in the business community, and if you haven't heard this expression before, remember it now. Commit this to memory because in the course of time, all retailers start to focus on turnover, in the belief that an ever-increasing turnover will keep everyone happy. This isn't so as profits are the lifeblood of any enterprise. Without them, businesses are living on borrowed time (or borrowed money). It is therefore critical for any business to get the balance right between sales turnover and sales profits. Reducing the price of products will usually stimulate sales, but at a cost.

Clearly, this process of getting the balance right takes time, and as we are always told, time is money. It is therefore appropriate that until you 'get it right' we look at ways of keeping the business afloat which to many means borrowing money.

If friends and family can't assist in the financing of your business; either for a new acquisition or intended expansion, you will normally be left to your own devices. Historically, high street banks have been the primary source of lending for small retailers, but this doesn't come easily or cheaply. How many times have you read in the tabloid newspapers that loans totalling millions of pounds have had to be written off by high street banks due to bad lending; more specifically bad lending to new start-ups such as the high profile dot.com disasters. Yet small businesses with seemingly good and profitable earnings and prudent proprietors are repeatedly turned away.

Let's look at some of the most frequently asked questions:

Question: Why do banks always seem reluctant to help?

Banks have two faces: one (illusional) created by a marketing company which serves the bait to potential customers, and the other (real), which is the face of general staff and management, and these people have to deal with reality. The former drives potential customers into branches whilst the latter filters out the desirable business and rejects the rest. Banks are at the top-end of corporate image, and despite banks occasionally going out of business, customers are so trusting of them, that they often commit their homes and souls as security against any loan offered.

In part, risk management dictates why a lender will, or will not, lend; and of course, the level of profit involved plays a big part. Remember again, that banks too are retailers. They, like you, the retailer, want good quality and profitable business. They, like you, have the discretion to either accept or decline business.

Strangely, business managers employed by banks tend not to be good at business in a general sense, but rather good at knowing which businesses to be involved with. In the same way, financial advisers are good at giving investment advice to their clients, and yet amazingly, still appear to need to work for a living, which in itself is paradoxical.

Clearly, if investment advisers were half as good as their advice would suggest, they would have made their millions long ago, and would not be hanging around just to give you the pleasure of doing the same. Business advisers employed by banks are not dissimilar in this respect. Novice entrepreneurs often view their allocated bank business account manager as some sort of guru capable of giving them all the answers needed to run and grow a profitable business. These days, sadly, business managers have had their 'gut feeling' or instinct – which may be borne out of many years of experience – replaced by computer programs.

These programs vary from bank to bank but in the main they address areas such as solvency rates linked to a specific type of business profile. Suppose you approach the bank as a new start-up wanting to specialise in selling flowers. The bank's systems will highlight the amount of risk involved and potential return (to the bank) for supporting this venture. The argument for deploying these labour saving devices is that they are objective. Personality, age and appearance don't form any part of the computer decision-making process. Of course, other checks on the individual will be done, but more of this later.

Despite the aforementioned, these rather idiosyncratic systems are not however, always used when dealing with the 'big-boys', where initiative still plays a part. They – companies that talk in terms of borrowing millions – generally deal with managers high in the chain of command and these managers use their allocated discretion in combination with liberal accounting practice to make decisions as to whether or not they want to be involved. Indeed, it is not unusual for these types of deals to be agreed, initially, on a golf course. The same senior management also creates a more rigid lending policy to be used by a bank's tiered management structure, which deals with the large volume of daily run-of-the-mill business loan applications. These applications fall into different categories, such as new start-up or established, and then another tiered scale based on the size of the firm, annual turnover and so on.

Mandates (authority) to lend are given to all levels of business account managers.

In general, as a small retailer, you are more likely to be dealing with a junior account manager (not necessarily young) who has limited discretion to give any real form of commitment, especially on a first meeting. Usually, the basic account manager will deal with new start-ups or small businesses with an annual turnover of less than £150,000, and will usually have a mandate to agree certain types of loan, i.e. secured loans of up to £50,000 and unsecured overdraft facilities less than £5,000. Above the account manager there will nearly always be a supervising and very experienced business manager with a much greater mandate authorising loans up to

£150,000 and then the Branch Manager who will have the final say on loans above this.

Mandates will vary from bank to bank but in general terms this is how the system works. If you have made an approach to a bank with regard to loan facilities and are told, 'Shouldn't be a problem' it invariably means that the person that you have spoken to doesn't object in principle, but needs the 'okay' from a supervisor.

Tip:

Warning - during the process of arranging any form of borrowing, you will be offered all manner of insurance products including life insurance, critical illness cover, accident sickness and redundancy and even pension advice. Most of this will not be necessary; maybe desirable but not essential. Always agree to consider this extra advice, and review your circumstances later; preferably with an independent financial adviser.

Remember, once again, that banks, just like you, are retailers. They have to measure the risk/reward factor. They will generally ask themselves – if we lend to XYZ Co, will we receive an acceptable margin of profit for the risk and work involved? Clearly, the larger the loan, potentially, the greater the reward. If half-a-dozen commission-earning products can be sold to you as well, so much the better. The manager who successfully brings home this sort of profit, will also be well rewarded.

Ironically, the process involved when organising a loan of anything up to £500,000 is no more involved than arranging the smaller loan. But given that a manager of a busy branch can only see so many people in the working day, priority may dictate whether or not you will be even given an interview. It is also worth noting that the state of the economy is a major factor.

There are times, especially when a country is in recession, that banks simply don't want to increase their exposure to any more risk than is absolutely necessary. In times of recession, *damage limitation* is the phrase commonly used, and generally this means only lending to people that don't need to borrow – almost risk free lending. Of course, no bank would ever admit that its most senior management has blocked all lending. They would rather make you believe that your application, ability, age or whatever isn't up to the mark.

"Let me get back to you!"....

In summary, banks may appear to not want to deal with you for differing reasons. Don't accept that a refusal by one lender will mean no lender will want your business.

Question: I am already trading very profitably with no borrowings – and have been refused a loan! Why?

One reason, which may adversely affect any application for credit relates to County Court Judgements often, referred to as CCJs. Most people at some time in their life will fall on hard times, whether the country is in recession or not. When debts aren't paid, a final demand is served. If the debt is paid immediately, no official record is kept of the debt. However, should the final demand be ignored, then a Court summons can be issued. Once the court has processed the summons, the debt will go on file. This information will be recorded by credit reference agencies, and kept on file for a period of six years – even if the debt was paid immediately to the Court!

From that day on, whenever you apply for any sort of credit, this information will be immediately available to all lenders, and will probably result in the application being declined. Of course, if there was a genuine reason for not paying the recorded debt within the due period, decisions made by lenders can be altered. In practice though, there are few acceptable reasons for being delinquent on a loan to a prospective lender. It is worth noting that most of your suppliers will have access to this adverse credit history (by subscribing to a credit reference agency) and will be used as a guide when deciding whether or not to offer you goods on credit. If you already have an adverse credit record, goods may only be sent to you on cash on delivery basis, or cash before delivery (pro-forma).

This information will help you to understand part of the process, which can make borrowing money a frustrating ordeal. Do not be deterred however – there are now many lenders offering finance to the self-employed that have encountered past debt-related problems. You won't find many, if any, on the High Street. Look in publications like the Exchange and Mart or the more specialist mortgage magazines. Brokers can be useful but always agree to a sensible fee before any work is done as they can work out expensive. Ideally, ask a broker which lender should be approached for your type of finance, and then approach them directly yourself. Many specialist lenders now only accept new business through brokers so be prepared to use one. If you decide to accept the services of a broker, never part with their fee up-front. You may have to part with the new mortgage lender's admin/survey fee but don't include the broker fee. Indeed, agree at the outset that an agreed fee will only become payable when a loan is approved and cleared funds have been deposited into your bank account.

There are many people that have encountered problems raising cash only to end up seriously out of pocket by pre-paying brokers for loans with amazingly low rates of interest only to find that they never materialise.

Not all brokers are crooks. But do exercise caution and take the time to check them out properly.

Finally, when sourcing a potential lending source, check out the internet. This can be a very efficient means of sourcing funds and getting on-line approval.

Question: Why does my business manager give me such a hard time when my overdraft needs renewing?

Overdrafts appears to be something which every business large and small needs, but rarely wants, due to the expense and nausea that they create, largely because of the fees and process involved.

Strange but true – you will probably be bombarded daily through the post and email tempting you to take out loans and credit cards, probably fee-free, with no interviews and same-day if not same-hour approval. Yet, try and get the same amount via a bank business overdraft, fee-free and without an interview, not to mention security by way of a mortgage charge on your home, and you start to feel like another person – not the desirable customer the mail shots have stated. It's probably appropriate to focus at this point on a common error which your friendly bank manager might fail to enlighten you on, and this relates to the use – or rather mis-use – of overdrafts. This oversight on his or her part serves to create the excuse for even more punitive charges on your business account, because you 'the customer' failed to conduct your overdraft facility in the manner to which it was designed. Cynical or good profitable work on the part of the bank? You decide.

Having an agreed overdraft on your personal bank account is not the same as running a business overdraft. Your personal account overdraft allows you to spend funds up to your allocated limit. These funds can be used for any purpose. They are not cheap, and tend to compete with credit cards where interest rates are concerned.

Business overdrafts work differently. Primarily, there are two types: secured and un-secured. Security taken is normally a first or second charge on your home, assuming that you own your own property and you have sufficient equity to use as security. Secured loans offer more attractive rates than unsecured, once again, because the risk to the lender is less. Should you not own your own property, or would rather not offer your home as security, then a higher rate of interest will be agreed with you. In the present economic climate you should not really be paying more than 3% above the standard bank base rate. If you are paying more than this, see it as an opportunity to switch banks. Un-secured overdrafts attract interest rates at 5% or more, above the standard bank base rate.

Business-related overdrafts are agreed in advance of their intended use. Invariably they assist cash flow and are used sporadically. For example, you need to buy considerable extra stock in October, which you know will sell not sell until December. You also know that if you deferred buying the stock until December it wouldn't be available.

So, you don't have spare cash to buy the goods now and decide to make use of the agreed overdraft. It is of course pre-agreed because you highlighted this in your projected cash flow.

In reality, you probably never did a proper cash flow analysis but you instinctively knew that money would be required and that's why you asked for it six months ago.

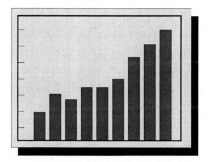

"sales forecast for the
first nine months"

This is how it should operate. Always ask for at least 20% more than you plan to need. Businesses can never build into their cash-flow plans contingencies to cover events like the September 11 terrorists' attacks or any other catastrophe, which can be seriously disruptive to trade. Other set-backs often forgotten or not envisaged at the planning stage are events like the World Cup Football, American Super Bowl, State funerals due to the death of senior members of the Royal family, the once-in-a-hundred-years flood and even personal immediate family tragedies.

Capital item purchases such as cars, PCs or mobile air conditioning (don't mention the essential holiday to the Bahamas), may need to be purchased and you see funds are available. STOP! This isn't why this facility was agreed, and when the overdraft is up for renewal/review in twelve months time you will have to explain to your bank manager why you need to borrow even more than you did last year.

Should you need, not want, to purchase capital items, make an appointment with your bank and agree an appropriate loan to fund it. If you want to buy a new car, ask for a car loan. If you want new PCs, ask for a separate asset purchase loan. This way your overdraft will always be available. Show your bank manager that you haven't abused it and it will always be renewed. I make no apology for repeating this – banks are retailers and they need to sell you these products.

A radical but often used alternative to borrowing working capital is the use of credit cards. This unorthodox option is recommended to the select few who can exercise great personal discipline. When the large American credit card companies entered the UK during the mid-nineties, credit card borrowing started to radically change.

Interest rates became tiered. That is, if you were perceived to be a low risk customer (you always paid your bills at the appropriate time) you were offered a low rate of interest. It you were always having problems or paying late, you were charged a higher rate. Not only did the market become more selective but it also became more competitive. One recent initiative, aimed at low risk customers, was the introduction of balance transfers, which offered 0% for anything up to twelve months. These companies know that having attracted this new business, at a loss, they would eventually reap rewards by relying on the human trait of 'being lazy'. That is, most people would leave the transferred balance and would eventually start paying a small premium in addition to the standard charging rate for having been given something for nothing.

'Hang on a minute – what if I simply transferred the full balance to another company which was also offering the 0% for twelve months deal?' you might ask.

This is a very simple and effective way to borrow money interest free. It is flawed however, as you are required to transfer an existing balance in order to receive this interest free loan. One way around this problem is to take a cash advance (most of these companies give free cheques) and repay it via balance transfer as soon as the statement arrives. You are then free to keep transferring the balance, interest free for as long as there are schemes being offered, and companies are willing to accept you.

Clearly, you have to be very disciplined to make this work, but the rewards are obvious. Apart from interest-free money, there are no interviews, no arrangement fees, no security is required and the agreement is open ended. Another bonus is that the fee and interest paid in the first month may be offset against your tax bill, if you can prove to the Inland Revenue that the loan is fully committed to the business.

One final, and positive, view on overdrafts. If your business is established and very sound, using your bank's money to speculate in your own business shouldn't be dismissed. In a buoyant economy, borrowing money at, say, 3% above base, to purchase additional stock, which you know will turnover rapidly, can produce a good return on your investment, despite interest charges. For example: borrow £5,000 to purchase stock that will sell for £10,000+. You have effectively made several thousand pounds in profits that you would otherwise not have gained. Of course, you will have attracted charges for borrowing, but, once again, the interest paid on this borrowing can be designated a business expense and therefore set against your taxable income. The hard part is knowing how much to borrow and when to stop speculating.

Whilst this chapter is dedicated, in part, to raising finance, there are initiatives which do away with the need to borrow funds for stock purchase, which for many retailers is their main concern, and primary reason for needing an overdraft facility.

For established businesses, 'payment plans' are becoming the norm. This system involves the retailer agreeing to pre-order goods well in advance of their intended use, and offering the supplier a number of post-dated cheques.

Fashion retailers, in particular have been doing business utilising this method for some years. Quite simply, goods are pre-ordered anything up to six months in advance, say £30,000 worth of goods, and then post-dated cheques are then sent to cover this amount in payments that the retailer chooses to make, within reason.

Payment plans don't tend to start until at least a month or two after the retailer has received the goods. This gives the retailer a great opportunity to sell substantial amounts of this, as yet unpaid for, stock in order to have sufficient funds available to meet the post-dated cheques as and when they are presented. This method can potentially remove the need to borrow money indefinitely. This system, however, isn't without risks, and the following two points should be remembered.

(1) Payment plans using the post-dated cheque method may remove the need for an overdraft to fund this excessive stock purchase. However, don't send post-dated cheques months before the goods are due to arrive. Banks don't always look at the dates on cheques being presented! If they are presented before the due date they will be processed. If funds are available, you will have lost them, and the associated interest (if you are lucky). If funds are not available, the cheques may clear but your manager will not be very happy and insist that you make good on this amount. Although banks can be proved to be liable in a Court of Law for accepting post-dated cheques before the due date, this will do nothing to help your long-term relationship with the bank, and the cost of taking legal advice and appropriate action will also cost a great deal.

(2) It is not unknown for large companies to present all of their

customers' post-dated cheques before putting up the shutters for good. Even major organisations can become insolvent at very short notice, and a last-ditch attempt to rectify their financial position could be to deliberately bank all cheques held irrespective of date. Getting money back from companies in these situations can take forever, if at all.

3

Buying Stock

Buy low – sell high. It is the law which governs a predictable outcome in retailing. It ensures success if you decide to play the stock market. There are two ways to operate successfully in retailing, and they are:

- sell goods in high volume and sell on a low margin of profit or
- sell goods in low volume and sell on a high margin of profit.

Selling goods in **low volume at low margins** is a recipe for disaster.

Selling goods in **high volume at high margins** is the ultimate aim for any retailer big or small.

The latter tends to be the preserve of chain stores and supermarkets offering own-brand products (more on this later). The former generally applies to budding entrepreneurs who have not done their homework properly. For example, selling goods, which are in low demand, in low volume, and to compound the problem – trading from a secondary area.

So what can you learn about buying stock?

First, from the products or brands that you have elected to stock, find out how their goods are distributed, i.e. by agents, wholesalers or third party distributors. If they are a Plc, get hold of the annual accounts to shareholders. This document often details what the company has done with stock it can't sell through normal distribution.

If the stock originates from, say, the USA and you wish to buy in any European country, including UK, discover by research, all of the European distributors. This is primarily for two reasons.

1. At some point, distributors of products will part company with the main supplier and for many reasons. When this happens, take advantage of this great opportunity to buy cheap in bulk. In this situation, distributors are very keen to do deals and clear all stock.

2. Each distributor will have goods which have been either cancelled by retailers, or goods which can't be despatched to specific retailers because they haven't paid their bills. Once again, this presents a smart buying opportunity and when preparing your seasonal buying budget, always leave at least 20% available to take advantage of these inevitable opportunities.

If you wish to stock a specific brand or product, you can simply approach the company concerned and apply for an agency. Assuming that this request fits in with their distribution policy, you will be granted an agency. Occasionally, your request will be refused. Should this happen, what are the alternatives?

Parallel importing, alternatively labelled the 'grey market', immediately fills this problem. Being refused an agency to sell something tends to bring out the worst in retailers. It is often taken as a personal insult, even though there may be no personal issues which have determined this decision.

Tesco vs Levi Strauss is probably the most high profile case of a brand not agreeing to supply a retailer. The retailer, Tesco, decided to spite the manufacturer by buying jeans through wholesalers in the USA and selling them on to UK shoppers, often heavily discounted. At the time of writing, the outcome of this case lies in the hands of the European Courts. The strange thing with this case is that it appears to have won the backing of the UK government and EU states. That is, anything which gives consumers the ability to purchase an item cheaper than the RRP, has to be a good thing. Good for who though? Manufacturers don't agree as it upsets tight distribution deals which, for certain products, are seen as essential for the continuity of the brand and the preservation of its image. Retailers don't want to see grey imports as it also undermines agreements for forward purchase orders by retailers.

Would you wish to pre-order £60,000 of goods from a single brand if you knew that your neighbouring store could end up stocking the same items and sell them for less? Of course, this argument will continue, as both viewpoints are valid. As a retailer, you want exclusivity on branded goods – why else would your customers come to you if this weren't the case? Conversely, as a customer – why pay more to one store when you can source it cheaper nearby?

So parallel trading does carry potential risk. As the retailer, you have to decide whether the risk taken justifies the reward. If it doesn't; leave it and move on.

Finally, the internet has opened up a huge marketplace for trading on a global scale. There are now many dedicated clearing houses set up across the globe that buy distressed stock; stock that has been repossessed, stock that has been manufactured and then cancelled just as the order has been completed and of course, end of line stock and production over-runs. These are not seconds, soiled or damaged items.

Once again, use your favourite search engine – enter the appropriate key words and start making new contacts.

4

EPOS Systems

EPOS or **electronic point of sale systems** used to be the preserve of multi-national department stores. They would pay millions (and still do) for large mainframe supercomputers and teams of analysts and programmers to create and permanently modify the software that runs them. However, for the small retailer, there is an off-the-shelf alternative.

In recent years many affordable and excellent EPOS software systems have become available and can be purchased outright for as little as £99. These programs are not very demanding and can run on any old PC. You simply load the software; connect a receipt printer such as the Epson TMIII-88 and a stand-alone cash drawer, which can be purchased from stores such as Staples or Office World. Finally, add your stock to the software inventory and you are ready to trade in 21st century style.

There are many reasons why even small retailers should invest in an EPOS system, so let's explore some of the reasons.

EPOS systems have many features. Basic systems allow you to monitor stock, create sales receipts (just like a till) and show a variety of statistics, i.e. daily take, weekly take, monthly take, bar graphs, pie charts etc. They can remind you to order stock and even tell you what your VAT liability is at any given moment. Supermarket EPOS systems are much more sophisticated and, apart from the above, can even predict trends based on past performance, so that stock can be ordered in anticipation of sales to come. I could devote many paragraphs to this but I won't because it's not relevant to the small retailer.

EPOS systems also actually also serve a more sinister task which is often unknown to employees. One aspect is 'Shrinkage' – the nice term for stolen stock – which, according to statistical research conducted by companies manufacturing devices to reduce shrinkage, is often more commonplace with staff than members of the public and can surface in many ways. Statistics show that in excess of 25% of missing stock is down to employees misbehaving. This is where any EPOS system starts to immediately pay for itself and can literally save the retailer many thousands of pounds.

Stock control is a big part of running any retail operation and is probably the main reason why EPOS systems came into being. If you are not familiar with the process, let me give a very simple example. On Monday morning, you take delivery of twelve long-sleeve shirts. Monday afternoon, you sell four. At the end of the day the system shows that you still have eight left in stock to sell. In fact, you don't have to wait until the end of the day to access this information. All EPOS systems operate in real-time. That means that you can check stock levels at any time of the day – even when goods are being sold. The over-riding issue here is accountability. If all staff and management are aware that the system will highlight discrepancies, they will think twice before 'borrowing stock'.

Tip:

Regular stock takes should always be done with a member of staff. This is to make everyone aware that all stock is accounted for, and that stock, whether placed on rails, shelves or scattered on a basement floor has been noted. Discrepancies should be highlighted and pinned to the staff notice board. Staff and management should be made aware that regular stock takes will be held, and they should also be trained to understand why they are held.

All EPOS systems generate a ledger. That is, a tabulated list of columns showing, for example: date of sale, time of sale, employee number, method of payment – cash, credit card – items purchased etc. One of the most important anti-fraud features contained within the ledger is the table column, which shows the status, such as sale, void, refund, cash-back, and deposit.

Large chain stores generate regular reports using this facility to highlight returns and refund patterns. Apart from the obvious, i.e. 'how much have we had to give back to customers today', it also highlights which employees have given refunds, at what intervals and for how much. Sophisticated systems can print an employee profile and match it against other employees. Should a particular individual give refunds in excess of the norm, or if a regular pattern of refunds should develop, alarm bells will ring. Many staff has been caught giving friends and family cash refunds on goods which were never purchased in first place. Whether a retailer chooses to proffer this information or not to staff is down to company operating preference. The fact of the matter is, that when these systems are in place, they work and are highly effective at doing their job.

What ever your aversion to technology – invest in an EPOS system. It will pay for itself many times over.

Question: How do I purchase an EPOS system?

The easiest way is to contact a local cash register supplier. **Easiest not cheapest**. Unless you are completely unfamiliar with PCs, don't do this. Cash register suppliers nearly always lease equipment. You are then nearly always required to buy the consumables: till rolls, ink cartridges etc. There is also the need to insure the item and lock into an annual maintenance contract (by the supplier). Clearly, it all adds up to a very expensive exercise (leased systems can cost well in excess of £100 per month for a single till!).

Do it the smart way:

- Log onto the Internet and choose a search engine, i.e. Alta Vista, Google or Yahoo
- On the search field, type: EPOS systems.
- You will normally get at least a dozen software packages to experiment with.
- Download the free trial version, install it, add stock details and practice different situations. Yes – you can run your EPOS system from any PC. Just add a receipt printer and cash drawer. If you really want to spend money, why not add a pole display and a bar code reader?

Most EPOS software is DOS based, and still is. For people new to PC technology, DOS-based software is pre-Windows. The good news is that most DOS-based software uses very small files, which can be downloaded very quickly, and most can be run under all versions of the Microsoft Windows operating system.

In my experience, the best EPOS systems are developed in the USA. Don't let this put you off if you trade in Europe. Again, most systems have the capability to utilise a lot of different currencies including the £ and the Euro, so are very user and multi-national friendly.

If you are not getting much from the search engines try the following site:

htttp://www.aposme.com

This is my personal favourite. Download a free trial version and use it for one month. If you are happy with the system, simply purchase a 'key' (code) on-line and continue indefinitely. No further payments at all unless you decide to buy further PCs (to create more tills). At the time of writing, this package offers free software upgrades, which become available from time-to-time.

NB – By adding further tills you can create your own network. That is, you can have several tills operating in different parts of your store, even on different floors, and they will all share the same database.

As a retailer, however large, you will not have escaped the customer who feels the need to demand a discount on a purchase. With never ending consumer TV programmes advising 'don't pay the full price of ...', 'always ask for a discount on ...', irrespective of whether it's a corner shop or Harrods, a new culture of customers has emerged. Armed with your EPOS, your reply – 'I'm sorry, but the EPOS system doesn't allow me to discount items' – is a credible way of dealing with such people without the situation becoming confrontational. You are able to empathise with the customer and blame the management for installing such an 'inflexible system'. Of course, this is totally untrue, as all EPOS systems allow the operator to discount items at any time. But if you feel that this type of customer is just 'trying it on' why not use it as an ally. For the truly non-assertive shopkeeper, this is a dream product, which also impacts very positively on profit margins

Finally, seasoned retailers are keen statisticians. They analyse (or should) how many people come through the door daily (some even invest in electronic head counters) and can then highlight the ratio of sales per head, by the hour and by the day. This is, or should be common practice. Large retailers would cite this as one of their key indicators. It highlights trends such as high foot traffic in store, and few sales – the economy may be slowing or maybe prices need adjusting downwards. Conversely, low foot-traffic and high sales may give scope to increase prices and inflate profit margins.

Some EPOS systems can link to an electronic head count system, automating the process of comparing footfall against sales. Even basic EPOS systems highlight what you have taken at each hour of the day, what was spent in total and average spend per customer together with how many items per customer were purchased.

After reading the above can you really afford not to use an EPOS system? And if you already use a system, are you maximising its functionality?

5

Trade Association Benefits

Warning! Do not overlook this chapter – the title may look uninspiring but you stand to gain massively by acting on the following advice.

Any country, which offers sophisticated retailing, will also acquire a number of associated trade organisations. Cynics would argue these organisations are parasitic on small businesses and are only looking to serve their own interests. However, search for these organisations as many offer some very attractive savings. Despite annual subscription fees, usually determined by the size of your store turnover or number of branches, real savings can be made due to the collective bargaining power gained from combining the needs of members with services generally required. These requirements are then 'brokered' by the trade body and deals are then done with banks, insurance companies, printers, car lease companies and so on.

Substantial savings can be made, for example, on merchant service providers. Merchant services (MSPs) is the label attached to bank subsidiaries that deal with the processing of your customers' credit and debit cards. It is a preconceived mis-conception that you must deal with your own bank's merchant services. Indeed, the option to change your merchant service provider is freely available to most established businesses. Should you decide to look for more attractive terms, compare like with like as some will charge high monthly rental for the PDQ machines (pretty damn quick – card swipe terminals) and sundry items such as thermal receipt rolls whilst others may offer free rental in exchange for a slightly higher commission charge.

Partners in crime?

Yes, your merchant service provider is actually a silent partner in your business. With the trend for customers not wishing to pay by cheque, and even fewer customers paying by cash, paying by card is the only remaining option. Ergo, in the very near future, all of your customers will end up paying by card, and so too will a percentage of every sale become immediately payable to your merchant service provider, effectively taking anything up to 5% off every sale! (and people wonder why banks are cash rich!). Other silent partners in your business will be the Her Majesty's Revenue and Customs (HMRC – the old Inland Revenue and HM Customs and Excise have been combined for a while now) (including matters of VAT). And you thought that being self-employed meant being your own boss – ignorance is bliss!

One of the biggest savings that a company can make therefore is to change its merchant service provider for one that provides the most cost-effective service. How do you potentially halve your commission charges? – enter the Trade Association!

To point you in the right direction, a small list of some UK and USA trade associations are detailed in the appendix, which can be found at the back of this book. Of course, there are many more to choose from, and these can be found on the internet. In fact, type in the key words 'trade associations' into your favourite search engine, e.g. Google, and you will amazed to see over that there are over 34,000,000 references to these bodies!

Still on the subject of merchant service providers, it is clear that any retailer switching its MSP can save a fortune. What if, you may ask, my existing bank is the nominated partner suggested by the trade association? A common situation and one that can lead to a positive outcome.

Armed with the information that a trade body has offered a discounted charging rate for all card transactions (be aware that credit and debit charges also differ) why not approach your existing provider and request, as an existing customer, that the same rate is applied to your account. The normal reaction is for the existing provider to offer these rates if you first join the trade body. Remember, the trade bodies and MSPs bounce business off each other.

Should this be the reply, insist that you speak to the department manager. State that you are an existing customer and that you are now aware of the discounted rates offered by the trade organisation. Furthermore, you are not prepared to pay an annual fee just to gain access to your existing services, at the reduced rate. And finally, should you not be offered the identical terms, you will move your business to another MS provider. Depending on the competitive nature of MS providers at the time, you have just presented this manager with an interesting dilemma – risk losing you and your income for good, or keeping you as a customer and keeping income, albeit reduced. Working on the premise that half of something is better than all of nothing, you may get your way. If you don't – pay the fee and join the trade association. Of course, if you are successful with negotiating a lower MS charge without having to join a trade association, you are still missing out on other benefits.

Apart from reduced MS provider fees, you will find that, by joining a trade body, you may even be given 'next day banking'. At the moment, if you swipe the customer's credit card, the credit may not hit your bank account for at least five days. Next day banking means just that – your customer pays for goods via his card on Monday and it's in your bank on Tuesday.

It is clear from the above that trade organisations offer great opportunities to the high street banks, including quick access to many dozens, even hundreds, of established business customers in exchange for preferential terms of business. This is the reality and the driving force behind the various banking groups wishing to do these deals.

For small retail independents, I would argue that by doing a small amount of research and paying, relatively speaking, a very small annual fee, this is extremely worthwhile.

Question: How can I get my own Store Card?

As a small retailer, the prospect of offering your customers a credit card with your company name or logo emblazoned on the front of the card may seem a mite over-adventurous. But you would be wrong to dismiss the idea. Another advantage of joining a trade body is the possibility of acquiring your own store card. I have already outlined how joint ventures work with trade bodies and banks, and the same initiative is aimed at the retailer via finance house organisations. Traditionally, finance groups that administer high street store cards, i.e. GE Capital, do so because the numbers make sense. A chain store with fifty or more branches will seem an attractive proposition to a finance house looking to produce, administer and service an 'own brand' store card product. However, Fred, the high street retailer of ladies' fashion accessories with only one store, would not get past the first hurdle. The cost to the finance house of creating this account would be high and the potential reward very low. So how do independents acquire such an animal as own brand credit cards, which historically have seemed to be the preserve of the multi-national or high street chain stores.

You guessed it! The trade body will approach, if needs dictate, a finance house in the following way.

'We have approximately five hundred independent stores which collectively turn over £xx million each year. 80% believe that at least 20% of turnover could be placed on their 'own' plastic.'

Faced with this potentially and highly lucrative proposal, a deal is done. Sometimes, a small charge is made to offset the cost of designing a minimum number of own brand cards to each individual retailer, but these costs are small when compared to the extra sales created by adopting this additional income stream. Of course, as the customer can only use the card in your store(s), increased levels of loyalty is another positive by-product of this initiative.

Should such a deal materialise, you will probably find the finance house backing the card also offering you the opportunity to offer your customers an interest free credit period for goods purchased. For example: spend £500 today and pay nothing for six months – interest free. Premium brand fashion goods, designer jewellery outlets and such like can all benefit from this type of promotion.

6

Winning Customers

Winning customers' loyalty these days is hard work, if not impossible. Twenty or thirty years ago it was not uncommon for a lot of people to stick with the same bank, same brand of car and even stay at the same in hotel in the same holiday resort year-in, year-out. If you think I'm kidding, visit your grandparents, and test the examples given above.

Today's shoppers however, are very street-wise. As mentioned earlier, they have been brought up in a culture where the media – TV, newspapers and magazines – encourage 'bad' retail behaviour (from the retailer's perspective). Every purchase, it seems, should be one to barter with. Not necessarily discounting items, but extended warranties, the right, even if no right exists, to a refund, and the classic, 'If I buy this – what will you throw in for free?' What then can be done to try and recapture the good old days of encouraging customers to come back on a regular basis? The answers, in part, can be found at the local supermarket.

Supermarkets reign supreme in this area. They have had the best part of thirty years to experiment and therefore have already adopted a best practice model. The trouble is that their business model doesn't transfer easily to the small retailer.

Small retailers clearly operate in a different league. Loyalty offered by customers tends to be very fickle and new and more inventive initiatives need to be explored. Own brand cards mentioned in the previous chapter help but this alone is inadequate, and more effort is needed.

You have to start somewhere, so why not start with your existing customers. These people have already been won as customers, and it is much easier dealing with existing customers than chasing new ones. One successful idea involves putting each customer's purchase receipt into a folder. Printing costs have dropped dramatically in recent years and full colour 2/3rds A4 folded on high quality gloss art paper provides an impressive and immediate vehicle to encourage repeat business. This receipt folder is not just an indulgence to spend money unnecessarily; in fact, whatever the printing costs amount to, they will pale when the benefits are explained.

In the first instance, one of the most stressful and major regular occurrences that retail staff and management face relates to the 'returns policy'. All seasoned retailers know that a percentage of goods sold will eventually find their way back to the store. You can't escape from this situation, but you can serve to diffuse this problem before it happens. Small retailers tend to have small premises, and as such, when someone returns with either unwanted goods, defective or otherwise, dealing with disgruntled, aggressive and probably loud-mouthed customers is less than ideal, especially if other customers are in the store.

It follows therefore, that this scenario has to be addressed, and in a way that accommodates most of the reasons for returning goods. One solution is to enclose the customer's purchase receipt in a folder, which, in simple terms, explains the options available should the customer decide to return the item. This simple idea is very effective because the customer has seen that your returns policy is 'not hidden', but clearly stated, and attached to the receipt. This creates no logical reason for misunderstanding, and thereby effectively removes grounds for confrontation.

This system works well because very few people admit to not either being able or bothered to read what was given to them at the time of purchase, and which, no doubt they are probably holding when they re-enter the store. They can only make themselves look foolish in the process.

In this situation, a potentially hostile confrontation is replaced with a positive, objective, harmonious understanding. This in itself is conducive to future sales, as, if the customer has understood the rules, and has experienced a positive returns situation, he or she is more likely to come back as a customer in the future.

Other sales opportunities can present themselves by using this same receipt folder.

When the customer is handed the receipt, highlight that bringing it back within 14 days will entitle him or her to a discount off the next purchase. This message can be written on the folder and will generate additional business within that timeframe. It will also come as no great surprise that a small number of customers will immediately make another additional purchase because of this incentive.

Printed either inside or on the rear of the folder will be your marketing message, which could take the form of 'return with this folder within 14 (or 28) days and you will receive a generous discount off your next purchase'. This variable message should also convey your returns policy, which should be printed inside the receipt folder.

Tip:

If your store is established, why not offer space in your receipt folder to complimentary businesses. Their payment will offset your printing costs. For example, if you are selling fashion clothing to teenagers, nightclubs and/or bars may wish to advertise on your receipt folder. Shoe shops may get interest from other stores selling accessories or even service providers such as chiropractors. These variables are unlimited.

Place 'price match guarantee posters' around the store. This is especially useful if you make this conditional – such as (and in the smallest print readable) *'price relates to non-sale items, applicable price match relates to xyz town only. Item must not be in sale or be seconds. Store must hold agency for product etc'*.

By emphasising the price match guarantee, you are offering reassurance to potential customers that your pricing is keen – even if it isn't! At a subliminal level, they see no reason to shop around for the same product. Of course, the receipt folder is just one of many methods to win customers, but selling, in the main, is a person-to-person discipline.

Many small retailers fail to understand their own sphere of influence, often only viewing new faces in the store as potential customers.

Retailing is about shoppers becoming customers. Therefore, by targeting the people that you know; including friends and family, members of staff and friends of members of staff you have potentially access to many, many customers. Visiting sales representatives, delivery men, maintenance men ... the list is endless, and they are all potential customers. View them from this perspective, adopt a sales strategy of identifying a need, and meet that need. See how quickly things start to change.

Not all customers would want to take out your store card but many would appreciate their own discount card. Credit card style plastic cards are cheap to buy, and a quick check on the internet search engines will produce dozens of companies offering this product.

Discounting product for the sake of it however, is not a smart way to do business. Be very selective about the way that you and staff members hand out this item. In simple terms, offering all customers a discount card, which may be 10% off all purchases, can hit the bottom line very hard.

A business turnover of £500K will soon become £450k. It follows therefore that a list must be created detailing why you would want to give out a discount card, to whom, and in what circumstances. It may be that you have identified customers that have made a point of only shopping at your store when the sales are on. This customer, if given a discount card is more likely to shop on a regular basis than just two or three times a year, helping, if nothing else, to assist the cash-flow of the business.

Of course, the card could be restricted to just certain high margin products or conversely just the most, or least, desirable products. The latter is effectively creating a loss leader in order that they may purchase other goods – something that may be familiar with supermarket shoppers.

7

Intelligence

'Become paranoid – it's helpful. Paranoia is simply a heightened state of awareness.'

Every retailer needs something to sell. This necessitates buying goods, which means meeting sales representatives from your preferred brand suppliers. I will emphasise that you must exercise caution and be guarded in conversation with sales reps. Most small retailers aspire to grow their businesses, and a great many are only too keen to tell the world how successful they are, and state what they are about to do, and how they are going to do it. A word of warning: DON'T indulge sales reps with your plans for expansion, even if they act like your best friends. Remember, they are also your competitors' 'friends'. Giving away your plans for expansion can kick start the competition into going one better which can totally undermine your plans and future success.

Of course, you could take a leaf out of the intelligence community's book by giving out disinformation. Stating that you intend to stop selling certain products to a sales rep, especially a rep who you know openly talks about your competitors' confidential matters, can help you to gain an edge in getting exclusivity on particular premium brands. I have known this to happen many times over the years. An example would be that you share brand X with a competitor nearby. By stating to a rep, who also visits your competitor, but who sells brand Z, that you intend to stop selling brand X, you hope that the rep will pass on this information. Often, competitors will follow suit believing that 'inside' advance knowledge and a competitive edge may have been gained. Of course, the opposite is true, and you could end up with an exclusive agency for that product.

Another ploy is to challenge your sphere of influence by attending business conventions and trade shows. You won't necessarily meet any new customers but 'networking' is always useful. Trade shows are ideal for networking opportunities. Talking to your competitors and suppliers can highlight inconsistencies, such as discovering what discounts for volume they receive and how much free point of sale do they receive from suppliers? The grapevine is still alive and working. Keep on top of events that will have an impact on your business. Remember another well-used phrase – keep your friends close, but keep your enemies closer. Senior executives from large corporations actually spend a lot of time visiting their competitors' CEOs – golf is normally a good excuse to conduct these meetings. Each side understands why this should happen. Both sides know that they know – but they still do it.

Gathering intelligence on your competitors is a good thing if you constructively use the information gained. Many sales reps suffer from verbal diarrhoea and when pushed for information, indirectly, will readily part with what they know. Put questions to the sales rep such as 'how much more do we have to spend to be on a par with XYZ Co'? or 'where do we feature as a business in the South East territory – are we in the top 10/50/100?' Your objective is of course to find out whether your competitors are doing better than you; are they more profitable; is turnover greater and so on? Only by gaining this information will you begin to realise where your business potential lies. If you then know that you are the market leader, how else can you improve? However, if you are told that you are the market leader, or number one agency within your sales region – how else can you improve? If you discover that your competitors in different regions are doing double the business – how can you bring your business up to this level? By asking for information indirectly you will always find out more.

Of course if you are really desperate to gain a greater understanding of your competition (and their habits), take a leaf out of the computer hacker's book for gaining passwords to encrypted sites.

Collect your competitor's rubbish! There is more than a fair chance that they will package this into neat plastic bags for you each week, for refuse collection. Who can stop you from wanting to help the environment and help the community by recycling more waste! Of course, some people would feel that this is being over-enthusiastic, even criminal, and with identity theft becoming a very emotive social issue, who can blame them for having this view..

Why not use more conventional means to glean information, and expand your knowledge? Publications such as: *Retail Week; Drapers Record; The Grocer* etc are trade magazines that are readily available (often by special order in bookstores) at regular intervals; some weekly, some monthly, others quarterly. These sources of information help you to check the pulse of your market. If business is bad, it can offer some consolation to read that everybody in your line of business is also suffering. Not necessarily good news, but it does mean that your efforts, or lack of them, aren't the main contributing factor to poor levels of business, and in these circumstances, a complete change of strategy may need to be adopted.

Don't forget to make effective use of the internet. Many of the large stores publish reports on-line; primarily aimed at existing and potential investors. If you stock similar products and wish to know whether or not your (big) competitors are either struggling to sell the product or, conversely, enjoying strong sales, search for their activity reports. Although many skim over the fine detail, just as many give breakdowns in product categories; often including brands and specific lines. Identifying these trends helps when the stock buying process begins, as a large company that has experienced poor sales in the past twelve months, may be very keen to get the business, and this is an opportunity to press for better terms, by way of extended credit, or larger discounts.

8

Background Music

Music – pros and cons

In a small store it can feel inhibiting and even daunting for some potential customers to enter. However, background music may provide a remedy for this problem. Appropriate music can create a positive atmosphere, and this can be witnessed more than ever in most stores around the Festive period. However, choosing to play music is highly emotive, and whilst the 'right' music can put customers in a happy mood (if they are dancing or singing, they're happy) choosing the wrong music can immediately turn some people off, and make them leave the store.

Many years ago, whilst on holiday, I recall shopping at a fashion label superstore in Florida specifically to bring premium branded clothing back into the UK. (Often referred to as the grey market or parallel importing). Judging the store from previous visits, I knew what to expect: huge choice, free parking, very helpful assistants, and of course very cheap prices. Based on previous visits, this should have been an enjoyable experience; sadly this wasn't to be. After spending just 25 minutes in the store I decided to cast aside our shopping trolleys, which contained several thousand pounds worth of goods and make a beeline for the exit. Why, because the new young manager decided that by playing heavy metal music through several hundred speakers each the size of a small house, they would attract a much younger customer base and give the store a cool image! I subsequently went to other stores (with a very bad headache) to buy the same goods at the same price.

Does this contradict my above reasoning about aligning yourself with the chosen group of customer? – No, but it does highlight the importance of getting the music right for customers in the store. I know a small number of fashion retailers who, having recognised the importance of playing background music and the positive benefits it can bring (sales), have actually changed music in store to suit the average age and profile of customer, without offending anybody. For example, on Saturdays – target market, under 25s – music played, anything likely to cause brain damage. Monday morning – target market, parents and grandparents shopping for their kids and grandkids – music played, anything mellow.

Simple but effective. Not appropriate for every store, as it is very labour intensive, but done well serves to enhance sales.

"spend, spend, spend"

The speed or rather the style of music played is also a contributing factor. Have you ever noticed that supermarkets play slow background music when the store is quiet and fast upbeat music when the store is very busy? Slow beat music has a calming effect on people. Store managers know that people attract people, and therefore, keeping customers in the store idling around in quiet periods is favourable, and therefore the tactic of playing slow, calming music within these periods is quite deliberate. Conversely, during busy periods, the idea is to keep the foot-traffic moving efficiently through the store, and this process is achieved by playing fast upbeat music.

There is, of course, no real framework as to why, what or when music should be played in a retail environment. Whether or not there is a need to play music at all is highly subjective, therefore what follows is based on my own experiences.

Factors to consider when playing music include:

- who will decide on the style?
- how often should the tracks be repeated or changed?
- what would be the appropriate volume?
- who will be responsible for maintaining the agreed rules?

It is critical to agree these rules before starting to play background music. Staff must be made to understand that the music being played is a tool that must be used to enhance sales in the store. Staff must be discouraged from bringing in their own music collections, unless the person responsible for compiling the appropriate tracks has vetted them.

Parental guidance is now a common feature on many CDs and usually this means bad or undesirable language will be included on certain tracks. If your store has young children visiting (especially with grandparents), be prepared to either jump specific tracks or better still, stop the CD from playing. Embarrassed or even offended customers visiting the store with young families will not be charmed by having to deal with this type of situation.

Choosing what style of music to play in-store must be by consensus. Don't indulge yourself by choosing the music just because you like it. In the first instance, canvass the views of your chosen customer group, i.e. if customers are in the age group 15 to 25, ask this age group for its opinion. Remember that you are looking to enhance sales by making your customers feel happy and comfortable in-store. If most say that they would prefer not to have any music at all – don't play it!

Okay – let's assume that you have finished your market research and now need to buy the appropriate style of music. However, before grabbing your chequebook and heading for the local music mega-store, there are a few things that you must be aware of.

Licences

In the first instance, playing music in a public place requires one if not several licences. In the UK you will need an absolute minimum of two licences, one from PPL and the other from PRS (addresses can be found in the appendix at the rear of this book). Depending on how loud you intend to play the music, and where (the field behind your store!) a third licence may also be required, a PEL (public entertainment licence).

Both PPL and PRS are organisations that ultimately serve to reward the songwriters, musicians and entertainers with royalties.

Playing music in your store, even just listening to the radio, or your own personal CDs will require you to hold the above mentioned licenses if your customers can hear this music playing. Failure to comply means possible prosecution, a large fine and the need, still, to purchase the licence/s.

If you are presently playing background music in your store and you don't possess the respective licences, beware. Each of the above organisations has teams of people who are based regionally, and their sole purpose it to check for compliance. Each organisation shares its database with the other, and therefore just buying one licence and pleading ignorance when you eventually get caught with just one licence just won't wash. These patrolling agents are generally commission based and therefore are very keen to catch people out – and that means you! So, as a final reminder, apply for your licences now – you are a very easy sitting target for the compliance officers, and ironically, the more you market your business, the more exposed you are to the local inspectors.

Free music

When playing the same CDs for around eight hours a day, life can become tedious, and if each new CD purchased is replaced at your own cost, this will work out to be very expensive. Why not consider playing free music! In my experience you will find that at least one music store situated close to your premises will be keen to offer you free CD music for you to play in your shop completely free of charge, so long as you are prepared to reciprocate by advertising the name of the supplying music store. Make it clear to your customers that the music presently being played is supplied by XYZ Music Co situated at XYZ street etc., on A4 posters, preferably laminated. This does the job perfectly. Remember to place these mini-posters in prominent positions around the store, because I can guarantee that the supplying store will make a point of visiting unexpectedly to check that you are keeping your side of the deal. Make the posters look professional, and don't abuse the goodwill offered.

You could, or should, also consider moving things up a notch by designing your own media experience. Most PCs these days come with a read/write CD player. Software normally bundled free (or can be purchased) can enable you to take a back-up copy of your music compilations. That is transferring the contents or part of the CD contents to a blank CD. Most PC superstores now offer many software titles, which allow you to create your own music compilations with little or no music knowledge whatsoever, e.g. eJay Dance 4. However, this type of software also allows any retailer to make its own in-store jingles. Voice synthesisers come with the above low cost package free of charge.

Once a variety of jingles has been compiled, inter-space them with regular music tracks. The effect can be unique and professional. Best of all, it's very easy to create these discs.

Why not consider bucking the trend. Just about every store now starts to play Christmas music supposedly for the benefit of customers and to generate early Christmas sales. All well and good – but from the middle of September! Defer playing festive music until at least seven days before Christmas. Many customers will actually be relieved by not having to listen to what appears to be, at best, the same two dozen tracks being played in every shop on the high street or shopping mall. It wouldn't be too bad if the music was recently created, but most of it is over twenty years old.

Carol-free zone until December

With the advent of ADSL (broadband), digital radio is available on the web and it is now possible to tune in to many radio stations situated around the globe. If you want to play Latino music why buy the CD when you can broadcast Brazil's leading radio station. Easy listening channels are few and far between in the UK, but Florida has numerous stations that only play laid-back relaxing music. This is cutting edge technology and, with a bit of imagination, can give your store a unique feel.

One final word on media played in-store. If you choose to play DVDs or VHS videos in-store, check that you are not in breach of TV licensing rules. In the UK, it is still possible to play your own material or suppliers' promotional material output through a TV without a TV licence, so long as there is no external connection. This rule may be changed in the near future, so always telephone the TV licensing authority for confirmation.

9

Own Brand Products

From the outset, most small retailers rely heavily on premium labelled goods. Whether it's fashion, food or power tools, with no track record, customers can only be won over by the magnetic appeal of the goods stocked. Newly opened shops will always try for the best brands; those with the widest possible appeal. Perception of these brands is that they will be guaranteed to sell through quickly and offer a good profit margin.

These sought-after brands however, are not easy to get hold of. Long established competition will not give up brand exclusivity on its defined territory without a fight. And here's the paradox. Brands with this level of appeal generally acquire this status because of tight distribution, keen pricing and very high levels of marketing. Eventually, product distribution exceeds the point were customers start to become turned off by the product because it becomes 'commonplace'. Shoppers like goods that are exclusive to them (excluding run-of-the-mill groceries).

Remember what happened to Nike and Levi in the eighties, GAP in the nineties. Nike in particular acquired a unique problem. It was successful for too long. The footwear was targeted primarily at the 16 to 25 age group. Nothing wrong with that. However, when these customers started to get into their forties and above they still continued to buy the product. Teenagers these days don't want to be seen wearing the same shoes as their parents – let alone their grandparents, and that's when things started to get tough. Nike is still doing good business but nothing like the levels enjoyed in the past.

Fashion retailers dealing in designer or premium labels know that certain brands can rapidly move from wish list to yesterday's list. Fashion retailers operate almost a treadmill routine of always having to fight for the 'in' brand only to watch it slowly go down hill. In part, this problem occurs due to over-distribution, and within the industry there lies a rhetorical question: 'what can be done to avoid this never-ending process?' Truth is – I don't know. However, there is an alternative, which steers away from this problem before it happens, and this alternative is to create own branded goods. There are pros and cons to generating own brand products and we will now explore some of the pitfalls.

Just about anything can be made with either your own label or logo – sewn in or stuck on. Of course, doing this properly requires sourcing the product in the right quantity for the right price, and this can be very difficult. There are however, options available that can take out some of the pressure. The fashion world has one or two secrets that I will reveal. Firstly, up-to-date-fashion garments are often manufactured totally unlabelled. Wholesalers purchase these goods and 'tweak' them with subtle changes, adding a small-embroidered patch here an icon there; and of course, having their own labels sewn in.

Amazingly, these very same items will then become available from market stalls to exclusive boutiques. The industry knows that the likelihood of a customer shopping in a market is unlikely to be the same person shopping in a high-class boutique, so this practice goes on all the time. Some small retailers wishing to produce their own-labelled goods will even agree a joint venture with other retailers in order to keep costs down. Consignments will often become divided post-production but pre-labelling, therefore keeping costs down and margins high.

A third option also exists, and is presently growing in popularity: Small independent fashion brands source suppliers to make their own unique products. However, in order to acquire this product they, the design house/fashion company, must order a minimum number of each item to keep production costs low. A catch 22 situation, as most small design houses can't get the minimums unless they have either very deep pockets or unless other stores have agreed to pre-order. So, the alternative is to share the products, which are produced un-badged/un-labelled in order to allow independents to have their own unique range, which is then badged/labelled accordingly.

Each manufacturing country will also have dedicated areas where own brand goods can be sourced. In respect of the UK fashion scene, there are numerous outlets in Commercial Road, East London and around Deansgate, Manchester that offer high fashion goods off-the-shelf. Most of these wholesalers have shop fronts, but will only sell to trade visitors. Whatever you sell or choose to sell, if you want to pursue own branded goods, opportunities are waiting out there. You just have to be bothered.

Of course, own brand products, whilst desirable, offer no guarantee of success, and with so many variables to take into account, it's not hard to see why. Many retailers have no option but to go down this route simply because all premium label agencies are taken by established traders nearby.

Exclusivity

Another motivating reason for creating 'own brand' products is down to having experienced double standards by your existing suppliers. For example, a company promises you brand exclusivity within a specific area, and then reneges on the agreement. This is a contractual agreement to supply you and you only. This agreement may be open ended or at least for a specific minimum period of time. It may also be either a verbal or written agreement; both are legally binding, although when disputes arise, the latter is preferable.

I know from experience that hardly a day passes by without a retailer somewhere moaning that a key supplier has done the dirty on them by granting their branded goods to a new agency/store very close to their own business. Naively, both the suppliers and most retailers are totally unaware of a UK legal precedent, which protects the retailer in this situation.

The actual precedent is *Dr Holly Martlew T/A Ballroom vs. GFT(GB)* – the UK distributor of Italian fashion house Valentino.

This case was conducted in the Cheltenham High Court, Gloucestershire, in the spring of 1997. The case centred on a verbal agreement to supply 'Ballroom' (a small retailer) with product exclusivity, i.e. Valentino footwear. Despite this agreement, the supplier subsequently granted an agency to a nearby department store. Dr Martlew (the retailer) took the supplier to Court and successfully sued for breach of contract. She was awarded costs and damages amounting to a six-figure sum.

Amazingly, this precedent appears to be relatively unknown to small retailers and even large suppliers. The level of ignorance which predominates within the industry is incredibly high, and the implications of creating a verbal contract between supplier and retailer – although significant – also appears not to be known.

On the rare occasion that a small retailer does decide to 'kick-up', a senior member from the supplier will reply with something like, *'Sales reps are trained to sell, and senior management don't wish to jeopardise this process by getting 'all legal' with sales staff. We are very sorry – perhaps we could buy you lunch and get things back onto an even keel!'* This dismissive approach has gone on for many years.

Retailers in general have very little free time to read anything, let alone having any interest in searching for legal precedents for every given sales situation that could give rise to creating a contract, as defined in law.

The above precedent can be very useful though, and can be used in a variety of ways. It is up to the individual, under legal advice, of course, to mention this precedent. Whether a brand should be sued for loss of earnings or whether it is used as a lever to command greater discounted products for the long term, should be carefully considered. Suppliers normally wish to avoid this type of high profile case in the Courts, as it could potentially open the flood gates where claims would pour in from other aggrieved stores

This deviation from own brand goods is clearly important as the above outlines the process which leads to this commonly experienced situation. As always, even if the supplier caves in and softens the blow by throwing some money at you, this undesirable situation is unlikely to go away. As you ponder what can be done to distance yourself from this event occurring in the future, your mind will drift back to the potential safety of own branded goods.

Your own branded goods are worth developing. They must sit comfortably alongside your other goods and, ideally be priced slightly less. Your trading name may not necessarily be appropriate to brand goods. So become creative and think of suitable names. Some will work, some won't. Be prepared to experiment and don't become disheartened, as, in the long term, your own branded products will guarantee you a degree of success, if for no other reason than the goods can't be purchased elsewhere. Who knows – if you hit on a catchy name, other stores may start to badger you for the suppliers name! Remember this – every brand on the planet started from the same point: an unbranded product! And – let's not forget the internet. Selling something which is exclusive or in short supply is always worth placing on an e-commerce site. More about this later.

Fact: Kangaroo Poo is a well-known UK surf brand, and was created at roughly the same I opened my first store. Although this name was created slightly tongue-in-cheek, it managed to become very sought after by retailers nationwide, and in 2005 the business was sold for over £1,000,000.

10

Store Security

Security in a general sense is all-encompassing, from the physical shell of the business premises and the stock-in-hand to the limitation of actual bodily harm to staff and employees. For the benefit of the small retailer, I shall only focus on key areas that I feel will have the most impact (no pun intended). Securing premises these days will normally be subject to insurer's demands. External steel shutters, auto dial-out alarm systems and basically anything that they can insist on that in truth almost makes the possibility for making a claim non-existent, will be made a condition of granting appropriate insurance cover.

First let's look at stock, specifically, clothing. It was mentioned earlier that, for fashion retailers, hanging garments uniformly with all hanger heads facing the same way can make the hanging product look neat and even sophisticated. Take note however, that many fashion stores have taken to alternating the hanger heads when product is placed on the rails, as experience has shown that professional shop-lifters can very quickly lift whole lines of clothing off the rails which are then dropped into large black bin-liners. For the unseasoned new-to-retail individual, this is an unexpected event. When planning a new venture, you tend to think about image, premises, finance and so on, and unless you have the benefit of previous experience, dealing with shoplifters tends to be low down on the agenda, and when the event takes place a very steep learning curve is initiated.

Shoplifters – the ridiculously nice term given now to thieves – tend to fall into two categories: opportunist and professional.

- **Opportunists** seize the moment. They believe that they have detected a window of opportunity and will make the most of it, such as when only one member of staff is available and she is tied-up dealing with customers, or an irate customer at the counter is tying up all members of staff due to aggressive behaviour. The list of potential distractions for even seasoned members of staff could run to several volumes. But the situation to the opportunist remains the same.

- **Professional** shoplifters however, tend to be more canny. It is not unknown for these people to walk into a store, dismantle glass cabinets to access the goods, steal the merchandise (dropped discreetly into a bag), and say goodbye to the sales assistant when leaving. Unbelievable? This happens daily somewhere.

  They rely, in part, on the storekeeper's clean conscious. *'It would be madness to attempt such a ridiculous act with staff around and no other customers. So ridiculous that staff believe it wouldn't happen and therefore switch off to the possibility; especially if, upon entering the store, the individual concerned makes some polite small talk.'*

  Professional shoplifters also tend to avoid looking like the stereotype image, which tends to be a baseball cap (conceal facial features and hair), scruffy clothing (normally doesn't meet the profile of your customer), trainers (fast getaway) and a carrier bag (to conceal goods) which looks like it's been salvaged from somebody's dustbin. I have experienced and caught both males and females (some pregnant), smartly dressed, well spoken and of all ages, stealing goods. The bottom line is: think like a security guard – trust no one, and you won't be disappointed.

Shoplifters are of course just people. Paedophiles and sex offenders are just people. Ex-prisoners are just people. Psychiatric patients are also just people, but with the advent of care in the community, and the closure of most psychiatric hospitals, all of these 'people' are potential customers. You wouldn't necessarily want to stop these people in the street and invite them home for a cup of coffee but when it comes to retailing, you almost have to do just that. It is therefore imperative that management and staff should always anticipate the worst when dealing with the general public. Okay, smile, be pleasant and courteous, but keep your distance. Depending on where the store is geographically located, resources should be put into place to accommodate the 'worst case scenario'. We now live in dangerous times, and violent crime, specifically gun and knife-related crime, is always on the increase. Caution needs to be exercised unless you want to become a victim!

Remember, the travel infrastructure in most countries is now very sophisticated and allows people to travel vast distances, plunder commercial premises, potentially cause serious harm to staff and leave never to be seen again. Remote village stores are just as vulnerable to weapon-yielding thugs as their inner city contemporaries. This dark side to retailing has to be managed so let's look at some deterrents that can be used to deter the would-be thief.

Stock theft is the bane of retailing, and a different type of hardware has been developed to reduce this type of theft. Security tags are commonly used and have been around for decades. If you don't presently employ this type of system I will explain the different types available and their effective use.

Security tags

Tags come in all shapes and sizes, but only two distinct types, and these are either electronic or ink filled. **Electronic tags** normally require a 'gate' sensor situated next to the exit. Items which are tagged and taken through, or rather past, the gate sensor will trigger an alarm. This type of tag is effective, but not infallible. Professionals have two ways of getting around these systems. It is therefore very important for the retailer to know what can be done in order to prevent theft, even though goods are tagged. Here are the telltale signs.

The first trick involves distraction and two people working together. One asks the sales assistant if the garment/picture/watch can be taken to the entrance to check the colour in natural daylight. The person then 'accidentally' triggers the alarm that, on most systems, has to be manually reset. Meanwhile with the alarm already sounding, the accomplice, having 'bagged' goods walks calmly out of the store uncontested. Distraction is the key part in this method. If you hear the alarm sound, don't spend too much time looking at the door, monitor your other customers.

This type of theft can happen just as easily in video and music shops, and bookstores, the difference being that the size of the tag may be tiny if barely detectable.

The second type of tag is **ink based** – a two-part system, which consists of an ink-filled cartridge, attached to a back plate via a long steel pin. Once attached to a garment, the pin must not be pulled from the back plate, but released by way of a magnetic device attached to the retailer's counter top. If any attempt to remove the back plate is made, the ink cartridge will explode and render the garment un-saleable.

Once again, this system isn't perfect. Thieves can steal goods with ink tags attached, and if they have access to a commercial freezer, freeze the tags – or rather the ink in the tags – and them cut them off without causing contamination.

Trends, in respect of tagging goods changes in line with the economic activity of the country. In recession, it is a fact that there will always be higher levels of shop theft.

However, shoplifting continues year after year not just in recession, and prevention is certainly better than cure. In most western countries, there is a curious trend taking place. Police numbers are generally down, serious crime is increasing. Crime is therefore prioritised by type, and I'm afraid shoplifting is now near to the bottom of the list. Its position is probably hovering somewhere between parking a car on a double yellow line and selling lottery tickets to the under 18s.

Detention

If you catch a shoplifter in the act and manage to detain the culprit, don't expect a SWAT team to arrive in two minutes to make the arrest. My own recent experience would be – catch and detain the shoplifter, dial the emergency number – wait up to 2 hours for the police to arrive, watch the individual being 'cautioned' (because it's only a third offence) and then file a victim's report. Of course, you will receive a victim support pack which allows you access to a counsellor, although I'm not sure if this due to the shock of catching a shoplifter, or for enduring the police process and frustration of the end result!

At the time of writing, the UK government is about to pass legislation which will make a first offence shoplifter pay a spot penalty fine. This is highly emotive and controversial, and is seen by many in the retailing industry as highly undesirable for a great many reasons. For example, if a customer is caught stealing and ticketed by the police to pay a fine, how will they know in the future that a repeat offence isn't a first offence, thereby precluding the thief from a Court appearance and a criminal conviction? If the system works like the parking ticket system, how else will the police recognise repeat offenders? I suspect that this will be debated much in the coming months.

Surveillance

Video surveillance cameras can play a part in deterring theft, and once again, at the time of writing, new European legislation coming into play and is set to wipe out the benefits of using video surveillance as a credible deterrent against the professional shoplifter. Similar laws are being introduced into parts of the USA, and as always, this will differ from state to state. It appears that due to a combination of agitation by civil liberty groups and the Data Protection Act, consent of customers must be gained in order to record images of them, before recording takes place. Of course, there is great ignorance on this issue. Both retailers and customer have very little, if any, understanding on this issue. Large department stores can just about get round this issue by using very sophisticated image blurring monitor devices. In simple terms, the images of customers can be automatically 'fuzzed out' leaving only the thief to be captured on tape. However, at what point do you decide that an innocent customer has become a thief, if you haven't gained permission to film them in the first place? It probably goes without saying that in order to do this you also need full time security staff watching the monitors, and floor staff apprehending the villains. In truth, keeping staff alert to the possibility of theft, and focused on security issues, is probably the smarter option.

Security encompasses everything and everybody in a retail environment. I have witnessed first hand the blinkered approach, which is only focused on protecting the cash drawer. With crime against retailers rising year-on-year, take a step back from your daily routine and question every aspect of your daily practice. What, for example, could be used as a weapon against sales assistants? Scissors left on the counter top is an obvious one, but what about the pen left lying next to the till? Whilst this is obviously there for customers to sign their cheques and credit card vouchers, aggressive thieves could also use it to stab the cashier. Start to look at point of sale and even items of stock as potential weapons. If you had to defend yourself what object would you grab? If you would grab this why wouldn't the assailant?

Prevention

Prevention is better than cure. Always take security seriously by anticipating the worst possible scenario. Raising the height of the floor behind the counter by only six inches will make an amazing difference. It allows small members of staff to feel less intimidated by tall customers and can also be very useful for keeping an eye on the stock when the store is very busy. Staging is very simple to make and can be created very quickly and cheaply.

Bleeding the till drawer is something that all big stores have done for years. Once again, you have to anticipate that you may be robbed, possibly at gunpoint! In these situations, all of the cash is to be handed over. By periodically emptying the cash drawer of all large notes throughout the day, this loss is minimised.

In the USA it is not uncommon for stores to have firearms behind the counter, which are used for self-protection. Pepper spray, stun guns and even CS gas is routinely carried. In most of Europe however, all these items are classified as illegal offensive weapons. Personal attack alarms can be carried and whilst threatening to make a noise, don't carry as much weight as threatening to shoot somebody, but they are still a worthwhile precaution. Police in the USA are always amazed to learn that their UK counterparts race towards the scene of an armed robbery with nothing more than a truncheon and handcuffs – what do they hope to do!

Ever wondered why most supermarket checkouts have a large piece of Perspex between you and the teller? It's to protect the staff and the contents of the till. The top lip of the Perspex is often folded at 90 degrees at the top in order to make you believe it's there for you to place your money or credit card. From the customer's perspective, this is illogical, because what tends to happen is this: the person in front is at the end of the aisle packing shopping, and, as the next in line, you end up standing in front of the cashier, thereby forcing the present customer to pay from the end of the aisle and not the cash point for which it was created. Its real function is to offer the cashier some protection against possible theft, attack or both.

11

Psychology

The black one or the white one ...?

We are referring of course, to retail sales psychology, which could be summarised as: what motivates people to buy, and how should retailers sell?

This chapter could have also been titled 'Selling' because in retailing these two are inextricably linked. Many, many books have been written on this subject, but I will endeavour to try and simplify the process by breaking it down into just five steps:

1. From the outset, we are looking to sell goods to our customers. The moment they walk through the door, they should be put at ease and greeted with an acknowledgement – 'Hi – how are you?', 'Good morning', 'Good afternoon' or something appropriate.
2. The customer's **needs** are then **established** – 'How can I help you?'
3. Direct the customer to the desired product and offer a **choice** of products.

4. (**Direction**) Ask, 'Which one do you like best?'
5. At this point, your final reply should '**close**' the sale. 'Shall I take these to the counter for you?'

As a proprietor/sales manager, you should know how to explain the difference between an 'open' or 'closed' question to members of the sales team. If you can't, then you have a big problem, and this must be overcome quickly. Sales assistants have to be trained to sell. First, they must be trained **not** to ask closed questions. If the boss doesn't understand the psychology involved when becoming engaged within the sales process, then neither will the sales assistant. Sales will still be created and business will continue to be done, albeit in a haphazard way. If you are not familiar with open and closed questions; remember the following (small children do – it's how they learn).

Closed questions prompt a yes or no reply

Do you like this brand?	Yes/no
Have you been waiting long?	Yes/no
Can I help you?	Yes/no
Do you want any assistance?	Yes/no

In contrast these are examples of open questions
How may I help you?
How do you feel about that?
What do you like best about ...?

Try and start each conversation with, How, why, where, what, who or tell me ...

Many people lack the ability to socialise with strangers confidently, yet around family and friends, they won't stop talking. But placed, say, in a new retail environment with new work colleagues, being told to sell items that they are unfamiliar with and also being told to walk up to complete strangers, will be daunting in the least. However, confidence will come immediately when the concept of asking open questions and using key words come into play.

I previously mentioned that children continually use open

questions, but I have observed that, as most kids get older their appetite for knowledge, in a general sense, starts to weaken. Parents will often observe that their teenage kids become lazy in conversation, to the point of replying with very few words (unless they need something from you!), and again ask very few open questions. Armed with the following option of (closed statement), 'I'm going out tonight' – compared to (open question), 'how do you feel about me going out tonight?' you can see how closed questions start to become more natural. Of course, smarter kids will intuitively know that by starting a conversation with an open question, it will involve some form of negotiation, and probably a better outcome.

The essence of selling therefore is to establish the need of the customer (by using open questions) and then match that need with one or more of your products.

Open questions make the customer 'open-up' and divulge their motivation for being in your store. It enables the sales assistant to guide the customer to the 'right' product.

Key words are the clues that lead to a sale

Customers fall into two categories:

- people that **need** to buy something, and
- people that **want** to buy something.

Most shoppers, especially females, tend to buy what they need on a regular basis at stores they feel comfortable with, i.e. the weekly shopping for food and drink. Then there is the recreational shopper. In this instance they are not really looking for anything specific. But given the right circumstances they will buy. Shopping in western civilisations has already become a recreational activity, and as with any recreational activity, there are rules. The retailer creates these rules.

Many people engaged in selling are doing the job because it's simply a job. They would probably be just as happy stacking shelves in a superstore or working in a library. Suffice to say there are many people working in a sales environment that shouldn't be. These people are often un-assertive and feel uncomfortable approaching people in case they prompt a hostile response. Not wishing to be on the receiving end of harsh words, they find it easier to handle this situation by ignoring the potential customer completely. They hide behind the counter and make comments to other members of staff, such as: ' I think its really bad when sales assistants approach you in a store and try the hard sell – I thinks it's very off putting.'

These comments are often totally unfounded as most genuine customers want and welcome assistance. The trick is to separate the customers from the timewasters, and a few open questions will generate the reply you are looking for.

Of course, before approaching the customer, it should be remembered that the path to selling successfully is invariably down to choice. Always try and give the customer a choice, and the 'hit' rate will become much better.

Example: *'Do you want the blue one or the red one?'*

If they only want to see the blue one – put the red one next to it and praise their choice. *'I can see why you chose the blue one – the red one is a little loud.'* You have helped create a sale. Giving the customer choice invites a purchase. Only giving the customer one of anything prompts a yes/no choice of reply. Always try for, *'Do you prefer style A or B? – The red or the blue? – The large or the medium?'*

Have you ever bought a pair of training shoes? Most stores will get the pair of your choice and hand you just one trainer (probably making you wait several minutes while they lace it. The smart store will always pre-lace the shoes when they are delivered and the even smarter store will pre-lace the pair of trainers with two different coloured laces; hand the pair to the customer and say which do you like best – *'the one with the black lace or the one with the white lace'* This is technically referred to as a 'trial close'. It assumes the customer is going to buy the trainer – the only decision to be made is down to which colour of lace. Naturally, if the trainer is uncomfortable or doesn't fit, you offer a different style. But the format should be repeated.

The larger upmarket jewellery shops always have well trained staff, and they know that the easiest way to sell you something is to start with a choice of product. For example, you see a watch for sale in the main display window. You enter the store and ask to try it on. Young inexperienced or untrained staff at this point would just get you the watch that you asked for. The smart sales person however, would ask, 'Before I go into the window display, which other similar watches would you like me to show you?' At this point the above process starts at the counter, where it's back to, 'Which one do you like best, the (brand A) watch with the blue face or (brand B) with the white face?'

This system of selling is not new and is employed around the world across the whole spectrum of goods or services being sold.

Following is an example of how a service provider, a building society in the UK, used to offer first time buyers choice in order to achieve a predictable outcome – the sale of a commission-earning endowment policy.

Running parallel alongside any mortgage is the need for a life insurance policy, and in days gone by this was always sold in the form of an endowment policy (you may own one yourself – many millions of people do). The choice was either a low start endowment policy or a low cost endowment policy. In this instance they were saying would you like an endowment policy or an endowment policy – the same policy with different features. Unfortunately for banks and building societies, this practice has recently become outlawed due to many endowment policies maturing with insufficient funds to repay the mortgage debt. The main feature being that monthly premiums differed – one affordable, and the alternative, border-line expensive. Endowments are still available, but the choice offered by lenders is now more restrictive. Incidentally, for the uninitiated, when lenders sell you an insurance policy, they receive commission from the insurance company. When they sell you an endowment policy the commission is usually very significant, often running to several thousand pounds, per policy. Now you understand why mortgage lenders only used to offer the same endowment policy with two different names.

This example serves to highlight that even the largest companies in existence know that offering customers a choice, however unusual the product, will enhance the sales potential. Of course, offering a person the biggest and best choice of product available will not put money in the till if this same person doesn't really want to buy anything, which leads me into the next issue of identifying who your real potential customers are.

Body language

There are many books dedicated to body language and, depending on your level of interest, these books range from a light-hearted overview to dealing with psychiatric disorders and mental illness. I am not qualified at all in the latter, but I can state with confidence that there are many aspects of body language associated with selling which have been universally accepted as the dos and don'ts of the retailer's bible.

The following traits associated with 'shoppers' are not meant to be an exhaustive list, but an indication of the most commonly detectable characteristics. The purpose, although possibly over-simplified, is meant as a guide in how to distinguish between true shoppers and browsers (customers or timewasters!), and I would highly recommend reading more on this subject, if for no other reason than to freak out your family and friends.

People shopping – by that, I mean customers entering your store with both the means and intent to making a purchase – nearly always tend to initially make eye contact with a sales assistant. For example, customers may, in a clothing store, walk past the checkout, and either smile or make a polite gesture to the sales person, proceed to the clothing area, hold up two items and look at both, seemingly unable to make a decision. They may willingly enter into conversation, and make statements such as, *'It's my nephew's birthday, I need to buy him a present.'* This may be followed by, *'Which one would you buy?'* This scenario happens everywhere daily. This type of customer is almost shouting out for help, and with a little nudge will make a purchase. This is the situation that the even the most timid and unassertive sales assistant should be making the most of.

In contrast, there are the 'middle' group. These may not even understand themselves why they have wandered into your store. They walk about aimlessly, picking up items and then carefully placing them back onto the shelf. This group offers potential, so don't ignore them. They may be killing time whilst waiting for a partner who is shopping nearby. They are already shopping, but with somebody else doing the spending. This is the classic impulse buyer. Look for the body language. For the most part they drift around with their hands in their pockets, then suddenly, they snap out of a coma and appear to have acquired a life force. They have seen something that they want to buy – this should serve as a prompt to the sales assistant that this is the time to move in for the kill. An earlier approach would have sent them running out of the store. But now it's different. Now they need mild encouragement, and of course, this starts with an open question.

Let's not exclude the no hopers. They nearly always meet the same profile. No, or evasive, eye contact. Arms folded, and sometimes legs and arms folded. This is classic defensive body language. It means stay away, or I'll bite. Hands in pockets also means, I intend to keep hold of my money – don't try and get it (although in winter, it could mean that they just have cold hands!). These people may become customers – probably when payday comes around – or they might just be waiting for a bus to arrive at the stop adjacent to your store. These are not people that you should instruct your work experience or junior employees to approach and practice open questions. They should, however, be used as an example of people not to approach, and to test your own theories on body language.

If this isn't familiar territory, try becoming an observer. Not only in your store, but other stores. Practice putting people into categories and see what success rate you have. (Warning – don't tell your friends about this new hobby or they may abandon you! Nobody wants a stalker as a best friend).

On a related issue to the psychology of selling, there is one other, and final, important aspect that I will touch upon. Human behaviour is incredibly complex and whilst I have highlighted commonly observable behaviour in the sales environment, there is one characteristic which once again pigeon-holes people.

Intuition

Successful sales people tend to run alongside the conformist in society. They understand the need to break the rules every once in a while, and that's what sets them apart from the 9 to 5 community. Observing traits of business leaders over a number of years, I discovered that they generally fall into one of two categories, and these categories are either *intuitive* or *academic*. I don't have an MBA from Harvard but I have worked with people who do. They in turn have told me that I am intuitive, and therefore, as they are smarter than me, how can I disagree?

There is significance in this observation for the small retailer as it highlights something that isn't necessarily that obvious, but it is something that affects everything that you do in business, because most if not all people that you encounter, whether suppliers or customers will fall into one of these two categories.

Intuitive people tend to more sensory, which allows them to feel whether or not something is right or wrong, good or bad in all situations and circumstances before they develop. Conversely, academics need to be fed large amounts of data before they will produce either constructive criticism or objective feedback. From this observation, I believe intuitive people make better sales people because they have the ability to make immediate decisions naturally without having to resort to weighing up the pros and cons of a proposition, thereby losing the moment.

The point is, in the context of the above, understanding yourself, staff, service providers and suppliers will help you to communicate more effectively. Throwing lots of statistics, graphs, demographics and so on at academic people will require them a period of time in which they will digest the data and then come back with a carefully considered reply. Conversely, the intuitive person will know from a 'sixth sense'; call it what you will, that either a proposal will work or not. Data are still important, but these will not override gut feeling or instinct.

Another common observation that has been well documented, particularly in the world of banking, is that most people tend to fall into one of two categories, either sales people or administrators.

In general, sales people are notoriously bad at administration, i.e. book-keeping, filing and generally being organised, unless there is a lot of pressure to do so. In contrast, the people that excel at this (administrators) tend to be very poor at selling, in part because I believe that the thought processes are very different. One is structured and rigid whilst the other (sales) is flexible and fluid. Across the civilised world, you will have encountered these people that are mismatched, doing jobs that they are not comfortable with, and this can be evidenced most in banks and building societies. To the best of my knowledge, no other type of business has tried so hard to transform people from being admin staff into sales staff. These people in recent years have been told to try and sell you something at each and every opportunity. For example, every time you bank your shop takings, you will be asked if you would like a credit card, personal pension, extra life insurance, car insurance, in fact the list is endless, and so is their persistency, because they are bullied into asking every customer these questions at every visit.

Many of these staff have had their lives turned upside down because they have gone from doing something that they felt comfortable with to a new and strange world of having to sell something. Of course, the end result is inevitable. These staff leave because they can't take the pressure of rejection, and are replaced, but once again not always by sales people, because who wants their banking details screwed up by a bad administrator?

Finally, the purpose of highlighting this aspect is simple – are you a salesperson or an administrator? Do you prefer tactile activity with your customers or do you prefer to hide in the office? Conversely, which category do your staff fall into? Have you inadvertently employed admin people to sell your products? Because, if you have, sales may be disappointing!

12

Staff

'..in an ideal world: the English organise, the French do all the cooking, the Germans make all the cars and the Italians do all the loving. Imagine what would happen if the French made all the cars, the Germans did the loving, the English did the cooking and the Italians did all the organising?'

The retail environment is no different. Staff are not an incidental requirement – they are the business. Good, highly motivated sales staff, who are well trained, can just about sell anything to potential customers, and they are worth their weight in gold. Conversely, unmotivated, poorly trained and under-rewarded staff will struggle to sell even the best products available.

Your main priority as the leading member of a sales team should be to ask yourself – do I employ sales people or order takers?

The distinction is easy – sales people actively seek opportunities to sell, whilst 'order-takers' stand behind counters and bag what the customer has chosen to buy. One is proactive the other is reactive. How many times have you ventured into a store only to be told by a member of staff that they don't know where a specific product can be located or when asked how something is assembled do they highlight, smiling, that they know nothing about the product. Who employed these people and *why* did they employ them?

Employing people is potentially a fraught exercise. Before attempting to recruit, you must first define the job – that is, list what the job entails – completely. Include your own expectations. Stating that you want a sales assistant is not enough. Gender aside, question which personality type would you wish to have as a salesperson. Introvert or extrovert? If this person will become your only employee, will your personalities gel or clash? Detail traits that you can't tolerate and build these into the profile. When you have completed this exercise – profile the person. When conducting interviews, cover the list that you have already created. This method is commonly used by large organisations and is a highly recommended format. Finally, always offer a trial period, and if this is successful a further probationary period, before issuing a contract of employment.

One area often overlooked by managers is – how do staff behave in absence of a supervisor? Behaviour goes beyond not arguing with other staff or customers or worse, and involves being made aware of their own actions and how they can impact on customer behaviour. Take note of the two biggest misdemeanours.

1. Food

Everybody needs food – even retailers need food. Whilst this may seem an obvious and unnecessary statement, it isn't. Why? I have wandered into many small stores only to be greeted by a smiling assistant eating fish and chips or pizza off the sales counter. I have witnessed these same creatures licking grease off their fingers before taking garments from customers waiting to pay. These same people also lack the ability to detect any form of smell. If they did possess this sense, they would realise that the boutique they have been entrusted with now smells like a greasy kitchen. Eating and drinking at regular intervals is a big part of living, therefore, make sure that staff have an appropriate place to eat and store their food and drink. (Also make sure that your customers don't walk in eating food.)

2. Grouping

Small retailers generally have small stores. Yet, you will occasionally see the sales assistant chatting to a group of friends oblivious to the potential damage this is doing to sales.

Let me expand on this. It is true that people attract people, and very few people like to walk into an empty store; especially a small empty store. Imagine this same small store with one or two male sales assistants talking to, say, six friends, all male, which just happened to be passing by. An innocent interaction amongst friends, maybe. But when a female shopper enters this small space and is confronted by eight males, it can be very inhibiting – even daunting – and she will probably make a rapid exit. The reverse equally applies. In today's world, females can be just as aggressive or intimidating as any male counterpart. The trick is to get the balance right. Ideally, genders mix, preferably ungrouped. Sales assistants should be made aware of this scenario which is very commonplace in small stores, and be trained to be assertive and correct the situation before its allowed to develop to the point of choking the business.

The boss

What about the boss? Everybody needs his or her own set of skills, including the boss, to do the job properly. As the manager/boss, you need ask yourself some tough objective questions based on the profile and characteristics of your business. You could start with the following and add to the list:

- ➜ What are my strengths?
- ➜ What are my weaknesses?

However, these basic questions can be found littering all 'how to run a business' books and don't really give much away.

Instead, list the traits and actions of a boss that you would welcome were you to become the employee. Alternatively, canvass the views of friends employed. Ask what they would like to see their boss do for them. The reason for this is simple – successful retailing is about giving the right people the right product to sell in the right environment combined with the right incentive to sell.

Therefore the successful manager these days does not crack the whip or pretend to be a superior being, an animal of the past, but instead becomes a facilitator. Staff need to be empowered to make and take decisions using their own initiative. Managers need to give staff everything they need to fullfil their job expectations, and trust plays a major role.

A typical scenario is where a customer is paying for items at the till, and halfway through this procedure the cashier notices that an item hasn't been priced (this happens somewhere every second of the day). Therefore, a process needs to be put into place to cover this situation, which leaves the customer feeling positive and not agitated. If the manager/supervisor is not available, the person on the till must have some discretion to give the customer a choice, such as: *'Did you notice how much this item is?' 'It's not priced – would you like to wait while we find the price?'* or, *'I believe that this item is £xx, are you happy with that?'* This sample of questions involves the customer, and the feedback given will help to determine the speed of the process. Many customers are very impatient at the checkout; a factor overlooked by even the bigger stores. As this is the last point of contact with your store, this experience has to be pleasant, efficient and positive. Once again, trust plays a big part when organising this type of system.

As the manager, you must learn to be objective and put aside any prejudice. You also can't be good at everything – what you can't do, delegate, and what you can't delegate, learn. You can't be bad at everything – if you are – give up now and go into politics or local government.

As a business owner or manager, do not lose sight of your objectives. Your main objective is selling profitably. You should also aim to make yourself redundant, but not in the literal sense. Making yourself dispensable should be part of the business plan, and achieving this status is helpful to the company and to you. Should you become incapacitated for long periods due to ill health, you can rest comfortably in the knowledge that your empowered staff are taking the right decisions for the business in your absence. Conversely, should you be in top shape but decide to take that walking holiday through Tibet (no phones) you will enjoy the holiday even more knowing that the business is taking care of itself.

The right people are required for the job, whatever the job. Larger organisations tend to lose sight of this fact when economies are good and available labour becomes scarce. In these circumstances, take a leaf out of the American way. Many American companies which carry a large workforce 'kill off' the worse performing 20% of staff each year. Whilst this 20% are immediately replaced, the remaining 80% staff fear being driven into the bottom class of low achievers and hence productivity is enhanced. This methodology may be useful should the need arise to motivate, especially when the workforce is some distance from your own base. However, this practice would soon fail when dealing with a very small number of employees. Of course, this information has no bearing on small retailers running a business but it does serve a purpose, which is to highlight one of the many ways that the 80/20 rule is used. For those who are unfamiliar with this – read on.

The 80/20 rule

This phenomenon was noticed by a famous Italian economist, Vilfredo Pareto (1848-1923). Logically, it was known as Pareto's Law, but now is more commonly known as the 80/20 rule. Authors have dedicated books to his theories, but in the context of selling, remember the following: approximately 80% of your profits will come from 20% of your sales. Conversely 80% of your sales will come from the top performing 20% of the sales team. In fact, when your business gains critical mass and has more than 10 employees, this theory holds a lot more ground than you might believe. Think I'm wrong? I'll bet that you wear 20% of your wardrobe 80% of the time! However, men shouldn't share this secret with their wives, as it would be seen as an opportunity to throw away most of their wardrobe and go on a spending spree.

I make no apology for repeating myself, but good staff is the most valuable asset of a business. In retail, they are, in essence, the business. Bad or poorly trained staff can turn off all potential customers and, unless you have the monopoly on a retail trend, you may not be around for very long. Conversely, good staff are self-motivated, focused, loyal and keen to help.

In life, there are as many people who only see problems as there are people who only see solutions. If you haven't already done so, establish which way your staff see things?

Rewards

Effort must be rewarded, and it doesn't always have to be with cash. Always give praise where praise is due, but don't overdue the superlatives or eventually your praise will become meaningless. Likewise don't tolerate slackers, but deal with them objectively. Highlight your expectations and monitor these on a regular basis. If push comes to shove, and they are still not doing their job, let them move on – perhaps to a competitor?

Rewarding staff and building in terms which ensure continuity, need to be thought through very carefully.

A typical quality salesperson would earn a basic salary and commission. I state 'quality salesperson' as opposed to a person that thinks she or he can sell. There is a big difference. Quality salespeople believe in what they do and recognise and take advantage of opportunities when they are presented. Conversely, the former are able to sell but do so with a different mind state. They will only endeavour to sell when the need arises. Perhaps when they need extra cash or perhaps the boss is spending a day at the store and the pressure is on to perform. They may endeavour to do the job, but it's never spontaneous.

Agreeing the level of salary with employees is always fraught with problems, and the whole process is highly emotive. Pay too little and they leave; pay too much and the annual pay-rise can start to drain the business. I believe that the basic salary for sales people should ideally be a combination of basic pay and commission (motivation). Beware of paying too much in the form of basic pay, as this can encourage some employees to switch off when a specific level of income has been achieved.

Commission comes in many forms – daily, weekly, monthly –

individually, pooled or company backed. To put some real-world perspective on this, pretend that you are the sales person. Realistically, what would you expect to earn? How would you like to receive commission? When would you like it to be paid? Do not assume that all people want the same. Christmas these days is pretty much expensive for everybody. Frittering away commission paid weekly or monthly to some won't seem as a generous reward. But paid annually, just before Christmas, to some it will seem like a dream come true.

Finally, ask your top sales person – if you have one – to appoint a possible successor. Many owner/managers are too busy doing other chores to even contemplate what would happen if their top sales person decided to leave. Assume that one day he or she will leave – because it will happen. If this person doesn't leave by choice, old age and even death will guarantee this event. Planning a successor is not unlike planning to start a pension. Do it now and you will be rewarded at the appropriate time.

13

Returns Policy

Customers occasionally return goods to the retailer, who in turn tries to pass them back to the distributor/agent/manufacturer. This process can be highly emotive, as customers don't really want the hassle of driving miles to a store and have to find parking, just to return goods, especially faulty goods. Conversely, the store-keeper doesn't really want the hassle of having to fill in a returns form given by the supplier, and also having to package the goods and then walk twenty miles in a snow blizzard to the local Post Office to dispose of the parcel; often at great personal expense. This is of course only an outline of the returns process, which doesn't include the verbal abuse given by the customer to the seller for having to return the item in the first place, nor the flowery and grovelling conversation with the supplier asking them to take back something that was acceptable on delivery six moths ago, but is now no use to beast nor man. So what can be done to help the process?

The customer (the shopper)

"Of course I'm happy -
I always look like this" !

First plan ahead. Try and list all possible situations that are likely to occur which can lead to a product return. 'Prevention is better than cure' is a common saying, and is never truer than when dealing with customers returning products.

For example, in the UK, many shoppers believe that they are entitled in law to a refund at any time after purchase by simply returning the goods. Of course, this is not the case, and in most countries this is not the case. In the USA, laws and byelaws vary from state to state. There will always be statutory rules but going beyond that tends to become the goodwill policy of the store rather than the customer's absolute right.

Printing your returns policy on the receipt folder has already been mentioned, and can help enormously. Placing a printed returns policy at the checkout helps, but few people take the trouble to read it.

Should the need arise to return goods, one of the first things a disgruntled customer will try and do is find the purchase receipt. After finding the receipt, and probably for the first time, he or she will then read the returns policy, which, as previously suggested, will be printed within the folder, opposite the receipt.

Tip:

This receipt should also be stapled onto the folder at the point of purchase. This removes the potential argument that the terms of business and returns policy were not attached.

Don't under-estimate the need to deal with returns professionally. The concept of 'you bought it – it's yours' mentality belongs in a prison shop, dealing only with prisoners. In the real world, people have the choice to shop anywhere, and will, if not treated with respect. All retailers want their customers to come back again and again, and it is therefore vital that you try and cover all angles.

So, let's look at what can be done to reduce the negative aspects commonly associated with customers returning their goods.

Space permitting, why not separate the sales counter from the returns counter. You may have noticed that some of the bigger stores even have a separate floor for dealing with returns; and for good reason.

As a seasoned retailer, you have no doubt been presented with this example: a customer, female, mid-40s, slightly neurotic, wearing purple and spitting fire, decides to turn into a rabid animal at the head of the sales queue, because she wants a refund probably for goods given to her by a second cousin, twice removed.

As she is the recipient of a gift, and not the actual customer, you go to great lengths, and probably take some serious abuse in the process, to explain what you can and won't do. Separating the returns counter, therefore, is a big step in separating the positive aspect of retailing – serving customers and taking cash – from the negative side of the business, which is possibly taking abuse and giving cash back.

Ideally, the returns counter should be situated far from the sales counter, preferably hidden from common view by soundproof screening. It should have a rope/rail separator suggesting that customers should queue in an orderly line, and finally a degree of space should be given, as given in commercial banks, to allow some privacy to the customer at the head of the queue. This system allows the retailer to deal with returns one-by-one rather than being confronted by lots of wild, loud people fighting for attention.

This scenario may appear extreme, but even small stores can be plagued with customer returns, especially after the Christmas period. If space is at a premium, it may pay to set aside dedicated space for returns after the festive period in the store as a temporary feature. Once the dust has settled, turn this space back into a sales area.

> **Tip:**
>
> Some astute small retailers have achieved success by separating the busy post-Christmas from the returns process altogether. They make it clear at the outset that returns/exchanges will not be dealt with until the New Year. Customers can be informed of this at the pre-purchase stage: by verbally advising when the purchase is being made; on their receipt/receipt folder; by poster, and after Christmas by way of counter signage and window posters.

In both the UK and USA a rather desperate feature developed and crept into the business of consumer retailing during the recession of the late eighties/early nineties. In part, this feature is also primarily responsible for many of the confrontational situations we now see in stores with customers and staff. This feature – REFUNDS!

The word refund to most retailers (especially owner/proprietors) is almost akin to a member of the family being told that they have contracted a serious illness.

Small retailers can ill afford to give back cash that they have taken, and it is therefore imperative that every step is taken to both protect the cash position of the business, and leave the customer feeling reasonably satisfied. Thankfully, the practice of refunds without question has changed in recent years. High profile TV documentaries showing people purchasing clothing, in particular, to be worn out at the weekend, and then returned Monday morning for a cash refund, has made the big stores, which were instrumental in creating a refund culture, now tighten policy. The knock-on effect is that the high street is now more or less a level playing field. Refunds can still be obtained from many of the plcs but the timeframe has been considerably reduced from what it used to be, and conditions have to be met.

The bottom line is to make contingencies for what will be an inevitable event, and to plan in advance how to deal with these situations in a positive way.

The retailer as customer

Manufacturers that are good to deal with, from the retailer's perspective, are the ones which recognise that the **retailer is the customer**. Many makers of branded goods in particular wrongly adopt the view that the person in the street is the customer, and that retailers are somewhat involved in the process by passing goods on.

This couldn't be further from the truth. It is the retailers who create the marketplace without which the manufacturers would have no credible method of distribution. Yet, time after time, suppliers of goods treat the retailer with utter contempt.

Many of these companies should either get their act together with regard to proper returns policies or try dealing with customers directly in order to acquire some commercial wisdom relative to keeping the customer happy.

Companies that regularly send out customer service questionnaires to their product-distributing retailers are probably the best companies to deal with when returning products. The following are some ideas of what could be expected.

Retailer's problem	Good supplier	Bad supplier
Product purchased failed to sell	Takes back product, credits or exchanges goods	'Sorry, you bought it - it's yours.'
Product faulty	Immediate credit or replacement	Needs to see item before making decision
Returning faulty product to supplier	Agrees immediately and gives a returns number and arranges for goods to be collected – free of charge	Asks for very detailed forms to be completed and faxed before issuing returns number, and asks to return goods at own expense
Once goods received by supplier	Credit/exchange received within seven days	Has to be reminded several times before credit given

This list is by no means exhaustive, and I suspect that you could add many more.

Don't assume that all suppliers are the same. If you are having a bad or frustrating experience dealing with returns, consider proposing some of the above positive examples to your supplier – you may be pleasantly surprised by their response. In the first instance, however, make sure that you are discussing the issue with someone in authority – a decision maker. Voicing your concerns with the tele-sales assistant won't get you very far. Aim for the most senior person in the company; be business like, and make a point of stating what their competitors are doing. Above all, speak. Forget e-mail, fax or writing a letter. Nothing gets results more efficiently than speaking to the decision maker and putting him or her on the spot. Writing has its place but should be a last resort. Business leaders prefer to respond to the written word because it allows more time to form an appropriate response which, if positive, can have conditions attached.

'We will be happy to collect your returns – however, we can only do this at the end of each trading season – the box used to return these items must be made of carbon fibre – the minimum weight must be 100kgs – goods not deemed to be defective will carry a restocking charge of 50% of the original value – etc, etc … apart from that, we wish you a merry Christmas.'

It can be seen then, that whilst the reply may only come close to expectations, asking is worthwhile. You perceive your supplier as more accommodating, and the supplier believes that they have secured further commitment, and of course, this can be viewed as a starting point towards a system that will be fully acceptable to both you and the supplier in the future.

Purchase pre-printed 'return cards'. These cards can be bought from most commercial suppliers; the type of company that you would normally purchase your sale tags and sale posters from. Attaching these cards to your returned items conveys a professional image for your company.

Returns are a big part of any retailing business. View the process from all angles, then try and automate the process.

14

The Internet

" I think I'am getting the hang of it"

I have devoted a lot of space to this topic because I believe that the internet has already started to revolutionise the way people shop, and potentially, whilst it poses a huge threat to some retailers, it paradoxically also offers others the greatest of opportunities.

I have the benefit of experience on this subject, being both an amateur web-designer and an established retailer. What I realised at a very early stage is the potential conflict this can bring. Let me enlighten you.

On the one hand, the web designer part of me felt the need to demonstrate a good technical knowledge and superior design skills. (Is this perceived wisdom or inflated ego?) This tends to lead down the path of flashy graphics, background music loops, form interaction, animated scenes and so on. As everything creative is subjective, I also know instinctively that not everybody will share my view on the end result, notwithstanding the fact that I think it's a work of genius.

The sensible retailer in me however, wants the opposite, which is a fast loading site, easy on the eye, and above anything else, the ability to allow customers to buy my products without distraction. Simple – well, no. You see, there are far two many 'web people' that want to do their own thing and aren't prepared to see it your way. Of course, you could always buy a book on how to do it yourself (I've bought all of them, by the way) but many books have been written on 'how to do business' on the web.

I strongly advise you to benefit from my experience. If you really want guidance as to whether you are able to trade on the web, or indeed can trade on the web, you should initially ask yourself the following five questions.

A Can I afford to spend a lot of time in front of a computer screen, and, do I want to?

B Would I personally buy on the internet?

C Could I expect my customers to buy my products on the internet?

D What could I sell and how much profit could I hope to make?

E How can I set up my own e-commerce site?

Answers to the above questions

A If your answer to the first question is no, then you may wish to jump to the next chapter.

B If no – jump to next chapter.

C If no – jump to next chapter.

D If you don't know the answer to this, then you have more to learn than you realise. Leave the internet alone until to have the 'right' product.

E Read on.

Before making a commitment to trade on the net, you must also understand that there are greater forces driving the use of the internet, and only a small part of the force is coming from retail consumers.

Web developers, web magazines, web ISPs, PC manufacturers, mobile phone companies, educational institutions, web TV and so on, are all creating and inflating the potential for doing business on the web. What is known is that some products lend themselves to being purchased on-line and some don't. It's up to you to be smart, and to sell products that the customers want, that you can afford to send, and more importantly, with new distance-selling rules coming into play, products that you can afford to take back on a sale-or-return basis (because a lot of it will come back!).

If you want to know what the top selling products on the web are, log on to the internet, type in the name of your favourite search engine, i.e. Google, and type

< Internet shopping top selling products >.

The following results are based upon 'key' words entered into a search engine, as opposed to the url (universal resource locator), or rather the specific website address of a retailing firm.

Travel, credit card, holiday, MP3, cheap flights, loans, dating agencies, ringtones, car insurance, cars

To a small retailer, the above list may not be that encouraging as very few of the most popular search 'key' words relate to the offerings of small stores. However, when you analyse the following top words keyed-in for gifts, it all looks very different and very promising.

Mobile phones, digital cameras, lingerie, DVDs, cards, books, jewellery

The following products are also big contenders:

DVD players, standard TVs, camcorders, watches, flat panel TVs, perfume, lingerie and hosiery, MP3 and digital media players

Do your products feature? If not, and presumably, you are still on-line, why not conduct some market research?

Internet trading has already claimed many casualties due to a combination of greedy individuals whose only motivation is to generate income at somebody else's expense and by employing talented individuals motivated by showing everybody else how clever they are.

The main ingredient missing from these enterprising individuals and companies is basic retailing skills. Are they selling what people want at a price that they would be willing to pay and in doing so will it be profitable? The short answer is no!

Your research on the internet for top selling items should bring up something similar to the following list.

Books, CDs, DVDs, highly unusual items, individually crafted goods, incredibly cheap goods and anything connected to perversion or pornography, or indeed anything which most people would be too embarrassed to buy over the counter, has shown that the internet is a good place to do business.

Conversely, general clothing and footwear, like mail order catalogues, have proven to be very difficult and returns are extremely high. Food purchased on-line and delivered to your home is growing in popularity. However, unless you are willing to compete with the mighty supermarkets, forget it.

Fast food is one exception, particularly in cities. Ordering your pizza, Indian or Chinese takeaway and pre-paying on-line for either collection or delivery is a great use of the web. Broadband internet (always on) is now very cheap and for this type of business is an absolute must. I would be very surprised to see any of these establishments not offering this option to customers in a couple of years time. You read it here first!

You will often read in the business press about big brands looking to increase their lines of distribution. Choices include wholesale/retail/direct to customer, overseas, trade organisations and buying networks to name but a few. The small retailer often only has the one store from which to trade. However, the web, if done properly, offers the opportunity to play with the big boys. Your pages can look just as impressive and so too can your returns policies. Restricting refunds on a store purchase is one thing, but returns generated from web sales are something else. With web sales, you can take the view that 50% of something is better than 100% of nothing. Of course, you can't adopt this policy with a bricks-and-mortar store without giving the shop away, because high margins are needed to cover your fixed costs of premises and so on, but in contrast, the operating costs of the web-based sales allow your customers to have this luxury, and peace of mind when they read your price match guarantee and full refund if not satisfied.

So, for the undaunted, let's look at a quick and efficient way of becoming an e-tailer:

First, buy/register your own domain name. WH Smith or Barnes & Noble will have at least a million internet magazines on the shelf. Buy one which roughly says, 'how to make your own website', and search inside the magazine for the companies that sell and register domain names.

> **Tip:**
>
> Many major search engines will only recognise TLDs (top level domains) by the extension **.com** (USA/UK) or **.co.uk** (UK only). Bearing in mind that you will eventually need to be featured in search engines (how else will people find you?), don't be tempted to purchase the extensions such as .biz, .net, .org etc

For example, your trading name may be Scottish Kilts. The preferred choice would then be, Scottishkilts.co.uk or Scottishkilts.com. However, if somebody else has already registered both of these domains, what can you do? As previously mentioned, don't be tempted to depart from the above naming convention by using Scottishkilts.biz. You may end up regretting it. Instead, consider Scottish-kilts.com. Many ISPs (internet service providers) have the facility to allow you to search for your chosen domain name, and, if it has already been taken, all other options (using your company name) will be offered as alternatives.

> **Tip:**
>
> Whatever name you choose, keep it as simple as possible, e.g. if you only retail bottled water and your trading name is Highland & Lowland Fresh Spring Waters, this could become spring-waters.com, or similar. (I suspect without even looking that the domain water.com has been taken).

After registering your name, you will need to buy space from an ISP to store and locate your web pages. This process is very easy, and is just a matter of shopping around for the best rates.

Creating you website comes next, and this will be interesting. Your options here are to employ somebody to create it (could be expensive – what if nobody buys?) or doing it yourself. Personally, I would recommend the latter, as there is now a way of cheating when creating your site. Like most things these days, websites also come in a box. For e-commerce, you need a box containing e-commerce software; and in the same way that you assemble flat pack furniture, you assemble the website.

Before going any further, let's look at what's on offer and, of course, costs.

Once again, access your favourite search engine, and type in, e-commerce software. You will be presented by a long list of top selling products, which can be downloaded and tested. Alternatively, visit the newsstand, and buy an e-commerce magazine. They nearly always include free demos of each top selling package.

Actinic in Europe is one of the most popular and successful e commerce software packages available (a free trial copy is attached inside the rear cover of this book). If this is missing, simply download the free trial software from **www.actinic.com**; activate the program and then select the look you want on screen by choosing from templates. Add a few business settings, populate the database with products and photographs, upload the store to your reserved space, and off you go. It really is that simple, and Actinic are proud to make this justifiable claim. I presently operate two e-commerce stores, and both use Actinic; albeit different versions, which are version 5 and 7. Both function amazingly well but naturally version 7 (the latest issue at the time of writing) is now even more refined, especially when it comes to configuring the business settings, and this makes the process of setting up a shop on-line pain free.

As a web novice, you may need help fine tuning some of the settings, but Actinic, in particular, has a very good support team that will offer help when it's needed. In fact their website offers a huge amount of useful information, including plenty of FAQs (webspeak for 'frequently asked questions').

To give you a real boost in this exercise, we have included a free Actinic trial disc with this book, affixed inside the back cover - no doubt you have already found it. Do try it - you will find that it is easy to understand.

You may need help fine tuning the settings, but Actinic has a very good team, who will offer help and support.

Images

The biggest hurdle when populating the database with products is getting the images of your stock/products. Ironically, you will find that far from having to learn how to design a website, you will have to learn more about digital photography, file-saving formats, and how to resize images and optimise them for fast loading.

Once again though, this can be made simple by using a digital camera and software. The process itself can be summed up like this: take photo, import into software (i.e. Photoshop elements) resize photo to required size, save photo (output as JPEG optimised). Having done this once, you will find that doing this in the future takes only minutes to prepare a batch of images.

So far, we have purchased a domain name, web space, e-commerce software, digital camera (most come with free software to edit images) for a total sum of less than £500 (UK) or approx $750 (US). A lot of expenditure if you don't generate any profitable sales, but very little outlay if you can work the magic of the World Wide Web.

I would be remiss not to mention that there is also a 'dark' side to the web, and I guess that in the context of running a business on-line the biggest threat comes not from competitors but viruses – or even viruses from competitors. Viruses come in many flavours but all share a common goal, which is to do a degree of damage to your system software, hardware or both. Before downloading anything off the internet, make sure that you have installed anti-virus software and that it is both active and up-to-date. New viruses appear daily, so it is no good borrowing a copy from a friend, which he probably bought a year ago, and hoping that all will be well. In the ultra-rapid world of the internet, just a single day without an up-to-date anti-virus program can leave you wide open to an attack, and it is imperative that you install an anti-virus package AND UPDATE IT ONLINE before attempting to view any web site, or open any email. My own e-commerce stores receive around three to five virus attacks every single day. Luckily, my (Norton) anti-virus software eliminates them before harm is done.

I have possibly over-simplified some of the detail, but this is deliberate. Information overload is commonplace in the world of web design, and to help you understand why, the following encapsulates the demands and skills required for good website design. In summary, a website designer (webmaster) must have an eye for design (layout) and an understanding of web source code, which commonly involves html (and its many derivatives) java, JavaScript, perl, flash, asp, cgi scripts and direct X.

Assembling a site involves the use of an editor such as Dreamweaver MX® (the top selling web design editor) and an image editor such as Photoshop®. Of course, some one-off graphics may be required, including the company logo, and this would probably be created in either Adobe Illustrator®, CorelDraw® or similar. Having completed the site, it must then be uploaded to your web space by way of FTP (file transfer protocol), which may or may not be included within your html editor. I could continue by mentioning database creation and the respective applications required to generate one. However, unless you are a committed propeller-head, I would strongly advise you not to attempt creating a server-side e-com site, unless you want to delay selling on-line for a few decades.

It would be remiss of me not to take this opportunity to state that FLASH should not be part of an e-comm site. Flash, for the uninitiated, is a popular authoring software developed by Macromedia, which is used to create vector graphics-based animation programs with full-screen navigation interfaces, graphic illustrations, and simple interactivity in an anti-aliased, resizable file format that is small enough to stream across a normal modem connection. In simple terms (plain English), it is the web version of animation. Whole sites can, and are constructed using Flash, and whilst they can look great, impressive and flashy, they do nothing to help you sell products. These sites do not always display on older versions of internet browsers, and they commit the worst sin, which is to dramatically slow down the time it takes a site to load.

If you decide to take the expensive route of commissioning a web team to create an e-comm site, do not be talked into Flash intros or other dynamic events. Amazon.com are one of the worlds biggest e-tailers. Take a leaf out of their book, and like Actinic, keep it simple.

So, on reflection, this overview should give you an understanding of e-commerce site construction, a recommendation of an e-commerce software package, which is the market leader, and an insight to the geeky world of web design.

For more information and a first class guidebook to this arcane world, read *Marketing Your Website* by Martin Bailey (MB2000)

The main benefit to small retailers for using the web is being able to reach customers that are outside of the local market. Although any retailer, irrespective of situation, is a contender to operate an e-commerce site, the type of retailers that stand to gain the most are those that either operate in a remote or deprived area, or those which experience wildly varying seasonal trends such as tourist destination towns and villages. The reason I highlight this type of trader, is because off-season, the business owners and staff tend to have a lot of free time on their hands, and this free time should be used constructively by populating the e-comm site with products and dealing with internet orders.

Let me expand on this a little by giving you an example. A typical candidate for an e-commerce venture may, for example be a retailer situated in a small seaside town or country village. Trade would naturally be seasonal and highly variable. Products being sold will probably be aligned to the local economy and therefore very expensive lines will generally not be stocked because a credible demand wouldn't exist. This same retailer may, if desired, be able to buy the top-end of products from suppliers and only sell them on the web, often without actually holding the expensive item in stock. How? A website is created and advertised, of course, in the appropriate magazine and these goods are then ordered on-line. The retailer then requests that the suppliers send the item/s direct to the customer's home address. In essence, the retailer has only taken an order and payment for goods that are not even on the shop shelf.

So long as the customer receives the item ordered, and at the price agreed, within the timeframe specified – everybody is happy.

This example may appear to some as unethical, that is advertising something that isn't actually in your store to sell, but it is a process that is presently in place and which in time, I believe, will become commonplace. Indeed, there are high street stores that have employed this strategy for some years. That is – you walk in, browse through a catalogue, and go to pay – only to be informed that the item is too big to carry, however, ' ... it will be delivered free of charge'. Sound familiar! This item is then delivered either directly from the manufacturer's factory or some regional distribution centre to your home.

Another key factor to becoming commercially successful on the internet is price. As previously stated, pricing goods for sale on the internet can be difficult unless you have the monopoly on a specific category of product. In fact, it has become increasingly commonplace these days for people to go to a high street store or shopping mall, and be sold on a particular item, for example a plasma TV, and then buy it on the internet.

Let me explain – when I say 'sold', I mean that the salesman has convinced the customer that one specific item, in this case a Plasma TV, wins hands-down over all other products within that category. However, although the salesman has done the selling, the customer hasn't at this point parted with the cash, and will often say, 'I will be back with the cash, just in case I forget – what is the model number?' You can probably guess what happens next – the customer, having been given free advice and a demonstration, happily logs onto the internet and searches for the cheapest supplier, which in all probability, is not going to be a high street store.

Indeed, a worrying new development in retail is starting to take shape, and that is high street stores are being used as showrooms to enable people to touch and try products without commitment, only to then buy the same product on the internet cheaper, and this begs the question, how can small retailers use this to their advantage? Answer: two-tier pricing! Maintain your full margin products in the store, and let your customers pay for the convenience of being able to buy the product immediately. Conversely, let your internet customers have the items heavily discounted. This is a win-win situation, as presently, many people are oblivious to this practise and tend to fall into one of two categories, and these are either tactile technophobes (only shop in the traditional way) or web browsers (prefer to buy on-line). Technophobes don't like shopping on the internet because they like to touch the product before buying (especially clothing) or they simply don't like using computers, don't have access to a computer or don't know how to use a computer.

Likewise web-browsers like to shop on-line probably because the most important factor to them is price and convenience (not having to move from the computer to shop), and not back-up service. This is of course a generalisation, but from personal experience I can say that this dual pricing policy does work.

A question which may have crossed your mind is how do I deal with the customer that has seen the internet price, but decides to walk into the store and buy it – for the internet price? The answer, in part, depends on what the item is, and whilst subjective, also depends on whether or not this type of customer would want to make the purchase at the full retail price. In truth, we have been running a dual price policy in our store for nearly three years, and we haven't yet received any negative feedback. Of course, this situation of dual price policy is not just restricted to small retailers and the internet. Many major supermarket chains have opened small versions of their stores selling, for example, the top 5,000 selling items, and these stores are situated in high profile situations, such as the high street and shopping malls.

Without realising it, customers visiting these smaller stores are being charged more for their products than they would have been in their larger supermarket stores. So, for the present time, dual pricing does have some merit, but no doubt this will change. Of course, you could consider having a slightly different trading name on the internet, and even a temporary address, which could be a storage/ distribution facility or even your home address. Doing this creates other potential problems, but if you find yourself needing to put some distance between your dual pricing customers, this is just one idea to consider.

eBay

In the context of trading on-line, it would be remiss of me not to mention the mighty eBay. If all of the above information on e-commerce doesn't tempt you to create your own e-comm site, then consider the alternative, which is eBay, the world's largest on-line auction house, which boasts a daily turnover that equals a small country's GDP. Although it is primarily an auction site, it is possible, as a small retailer, to offer goods that can be purchased instantly by prospective customers, and even allow you to acquire your own dedicated eBay store. The process is fairly simple: sign-up for an account, enter a description of your product, quote a price and attach an image; sit back and wait for customers. Customers can either bid for the product or purchase it outright, depending on the options you have allowed. Your customers can then pay, optionally, online through eBay's subsidiary paypal by either credit or debit card. This very simple overview highlights the process involved, but as in the bricks-and-mortar world of retailing, success isn't guaranteed. The criterion that applies to running your own e-commerce site also applies to successful selling on eBay. That is, your product must be well priced (cheap), very rare – or a combination of the two – and must be delivered within expectations.

A final note on eBay – a relatively new concept involves companies large and small utilising eBay as a clearance house for surplus stock. Until recently, auction style houses didn't feature as a credible means of distribution. However, with the advent of eBay, major mobile phone operators, high street electrical chain stores and distributors of premium branded goods are all starting to look at eBay with a different set of eyes, and you, the small retailer, should sit up and take note. In the very recent past, unsold stock, end-of-lines, repossessed stock and slow moving lines created serious problems for big manufacturers and distributors. Their options were always restricted, and mainly consisted of heavily discounting product and selling it to existing stockists (not desirable), 'dumping' stock in eastern block countries, de-badging stock and selling it on to small traders or, worst, committing stock for recycling.

Small retailers share some of these problems. How many times have you bought stock at a price level knowingly beyond your target market? At some point, all retailers are guilty of this. It's human nature to buy products beyond the means available, and buyers are only human.

For example, you may stock a range of technical jackets in the autumn/winter, which sell well in the price bracket of £150 to £175. You know this market well because you have been repeating this exercise for a number of years. In September, new jackets arrive, which are superior in both style and quality (according to your buyer), and these retail for £250 to £325. Everybody likes them, including customers, but nobody can really afford to buy them. You may sell a few but not all, and this is were eBay can be an ally. Goods like these are highly desirable to people with a high level of disposable income, and you should at the very least recover the cost of purchasing the item, and at best make a margin of profit. In summary, eBay allows you to become more adventurous with your buying, by allowing you an escape route when expensive 'purchase' mistakes are made. By playing this game, you are effectively targeting a different class of customer, which may open up new trading patterns for the future.

In previous chapters we looked at two different ways of doing business, and just to remind you they were:

- selling goods in **low volume on a high margin** or
- selling goods in **high volume on a low margin**.

By operating part of your business on the internet, you can effectively combine both formats. Supermarkets are presently the dominant force in retailing because they offer the cheapest prices in well-presented stores. However, supermarket sales assistants, in the main, have very little technical knowledge when it comes to advice on non-food items such as electronic goods, footwear, clothing, book authors, and all other non-food products, and this is where they tend to fall down.

You do need to be aware that, in the UK, there are legal implications when trading on the net, and whilst the following list is far from exhaustive, I feel the need to highlight the following.

• If you are taking customers' details, i.e. name, address, telephone numbers and credit card details, you may have to register with **www.informationcommissioner.gov.uk.**

  This is a government body that enforces the Data Protection Act, and administers the applications. At the time of writing there is an online facility to check whether or not you need apply, and many other topics relating to the DPA. If you don't comply, you may be committing a criminal offence!

• Retailers try very hard to win customers, and having got the customer to part with cash (or credit card details), no sane retailer wants to hand back the cash. A recent, and illegal, trend has started to come into play in the UK whereby a small number e-tailers have tried to make money from legitimate returns, by way of charging a re-stocking fee. I must emphasise, that whilst this may be seen to be a smart, albeit underhand, way of generating income for nothing, the distance selling regulations make it quite clear that this practice is illegal.

• You should also be aware that the Disability & Discrimination Act states that your website must be accessible to partially-sighted users, and offer other visitors who may not be able to use standard web browsers. Actinic incidentally meets all of this criteria.

• Finally, and as previously mentioned, by adopting a strategy of dual pricing (not dual standards), supermarkets can be brought to heel by small retailers. Small retailers can offer on the one hand a premium level of customer service to customers who don't mind paying a little extra for the benefit of this technical knowledge and 'special attention', and on the other, they can offer bargain hunters no personal interaction, but a promptly delivered and well priced box. Whatever prejudice you may hold about trading on the internet – lose it or lose out! Forget creating an online brochure, i.e. who we are, where we can be found, what we sell etc. Make sure that from day one you commit yourself to actually selling a product on-line. Static online brochures/adverts may have been useful to generate sales five years ago, but these days they are totally ineffective. To do the job effectively, it's e-comm or nothing.

15

Self-employed Status or Business Person?

Do you ever wonder how a person with a small shop ends up with a chain of shops? One of the biggest roadblocks, which can hinder progress for small retailers, is not always related to money, or lack of it, but a state of mind. It is true that every person on the planet is a gambler, as every time you cross the road, catch a plane or get onto a pushbike you are gambling that no serious harm will come to you. This might not seem like a gamble, and yet every minute of the day somebody on our planet will die whilst commuting from a to b. People also gamble financially.

Even people who manage to convince themselves that they don't gamble do in fact gamble, often without realising. By simply putting cash into a building society deposit account or mutual savings bond, people are gambling that their hard-earned cash will keep up with inflation, and of course, it rarely does. In order to keep up with, and exceed, inflation people (investors) start to speculate by taking a little more risk. There are of course many ways to invest, and quite possibly the worst place to keep your cash is in a deposit account for the aforementioned reason.

At the opposite end of the investment spectrum, we have betting on horses and the national lottery, but as you probably know this comes with the greatest degree of risk, and in contrast, will rarely improve finances, and can quickly wipe you out. So from this we can see that accepting too little risk is almost as bad as taking on too much risk. The latter can make you poor very quickly whilst the former will make you poor eventually.

Your own view of risk-taking is highly relevant if you wish to expand from what you are now (in business) to how you would wish to be. In order to understand the necessary state of mind needed, you must first place yourself into one of two categories, which are self-employed or business person.

Most, if not all, retailers are placed in the category of being self-employed, and with this status (as opposed to being an employee) probably contemplate, at some point in time, becoming very wealthy. For most, this is true, as why else would anyone in their right mind give up job security, a guaranteed pay cheque, paid holiday entitlement and all the other benefits such as childcare and pensions, to jump into the unknown world of being self-employed.

Having initially summoned up the courage to taking the big step towards self-employment, there will be many thoughts taking up your spare time, but in ignorance, little thought will be given to thinking beyond the initial business start-up period. For most of the time you will be preoccupied thinking about the level of commitment you are willing to take, as you are in effect, gambling with your immediate future. The stakes are high: opening your new venture in high street premises with huge overheads can rapidly become a make-or-break scenario. Conversely, opening your store in a secondary position will keep fixed costs such as rent and rates down to psychologically manageable levels, but will your potential customers take the trouble to stray from the mainstream to visit? And is the high street, and associated high rent, really that expensive if you can guarantee a high level of foot-traffic?

Getting back to the point, it is clear that very few people entering the world of retailing are true business people. In part, this lack of foresight and lack of forward planning is the main distinction between the businessman and the 'average retailer'. One is looking for unlimited financial success, by making a killing, and the other is initially seeking to make a living. The latter may believe that unlimited financial success awaits them, but this is merely self-delusion and wishful thinking. It must be remembered as well that there is also something of a paradox about retailing, in so far as a small business rarely survives and continues as a small business. It must either evolve and grow steadily over a period of time or be ravaged by competition. The notion, by some, that trading in the same format, in the same way, long term, year after year, is sustainable is simply not true. Yet many newcomers to retailing never look beyond their first year or two of trading. The true business person will have thought through the shelf life of the business, calculated his or her capital return on investment, and planned an exit strategy. In contrast, the new-to-be retailer will be more focused on surviving the first year, and hoping to survive in subsequent years.

So, before differentiating yourself as either a self-employed person engaged in retailing or businessman (to save offence, please interpret the word businessman to also refer to businesswoman), we need to first dwell on the term 'self-employed' running his or her own business and fully understand its true meaning.

Whilst this article is aimed at retailers, many professions enjoy the status of being self-employed, and for example most tradesmen are self employed, i.e. bricklayers, plasterers, carpenters and decorators; even though they may arrive at your premises or home under the umbrella name of a large firm, most are technically self-employed. That is, they are paid an agreed hourly rate, but many are themselves responsible for their own bookkeeping, tax returns, vehicles and so on.

At the other end of the self-employed spectrum are technicians often referred to as professionals. These comprise accountants, lawyers, dentists, surgeons and such – I personally refer to them as technicians because, in my view, they simply offer a technical service for a stated fee. Most, if not all, can be found in the yellow pages. They will do as they are instructed, so long as they are paid, and so long as your request is within the law. Incidentally, businessmen do not advertise in the yellow pages!

These, as previously mentioned are self-employed people running their own businesses, but few are really businessmen. They are self-employed and probably enjoy making a good living, but the main difference between their self-employed status, and businessmen status, is in part, understanding their optimum earning power available, and personal involvement with customers. If you are self-employed and actually deal with customers yourself, then you have really created a job for yourself but with self-employed status. You have chosen a path that will limit your earning capacity from day one. Even the dentist, doctor or lawyer who has chosen to work with patients or clients will have restricted their income-earning capacity, simply because they too have chosen to be self-employed technicians, and not self-employed business people.

In contrast, businessmen apply a different mindset, and if success is on their side, can enjoy unlimited wealth. Businessman may be dentists, doctors, and lawyers and yes, just like you retailers, but they have recognised that by dealing with their customers directly, this restricts them from growing their own businesses, which in turn restricts their earning potential. Businessmen therefore try to put some distance between themselves and their customers and focus more on strategy and development. Your ultimate aim therefore, if you are ambitious and wish to move from self-employed retailer to self-employed businessman, is to nominate members of staff with the key skills required to manage your business effectively in your absence. When, and only when, you have achieved this optimum level of efficiency, should you start building your empire, by opening additional stores. This process is then repeated until you have acquired a manageable number of units.

Depending on your aspirations, your aim as an established small retailer should be to grow your business, as opposed to being destroyed by competition, and this can be achieved by developing your management skills and ultimately learning what it means to delegate. Freeing yourself from day to day routine is the key to properly developing and growing your business. Indeed, really knowing whether or not you have become a true 'businessman' can be judged by asking yourself the following question: 'If I went on holiday for six months, would I still return to a profitable and thriving business?' If you can answer yes, congratulations. If you can't or you are at least doubtful, then you have work to do on the systems currently employed.

So, if you are to migrate from being self-employed to

businessman, how do you manage growth? and how many staff can you handle without becoming overly stressed?

Actually growing your business cannot be explained in this small chapter, but this subject will be dealt with in greater detail in *Big Ideas for Small Retailers 2*. However, we can briefly focus on the issue of staff management by, as always, over-simplifying the process:

Over 2,000 years ago, the ancient Roman army officers understood man management very well, and even today their efficient methodology is still used around the globe. Take the following examples:

MILITARY	CIVILIAN
One NCO to 10 soldiers	One manager to 10 sales assistants
One Commanding Officer to 10 NCOs –	One Regional Manager to 10 Store Managers
One General to 10 Sen Officers	1 National Sales Manager to 10 Regional Managers

Team leader / subordinates ratio 1 : 10

This is optimum staff management, and however big your business becomes, you will do well to remember this formula. These days, the early Roman rules of man management tend to either not be known by newcomers to big business, or deliberately ignored by seasoned 'top dogs', who do know, but in an effort to reduce operating costs (wages), pretend not to know any better. This short-sighted policy often makes people work harder, but not necessarily work efficiently.

This very short overview simply serves to highlight that, should you decide to properly staff your growing business, the management structure/ratio outlined above would serve you well.

So in summary, being a self-employed retailer doesn't necessarily mean that you are a businessman in the true sense of the meaning. Should you harbour the desire to become a 'businessman' I hope that this chapter has at least made you aware of key and fundamental issues that may be holding you back. Quite often, the realisation that your operating systems employed are woefully inadequate, and that the quality of staff recruited fall short of the mark, can allow you take corrective action. (Remember – could you go on holiday for six months and return to a healthy business?)

When, and only when, your systems, staff and store are operating efficiently and optimally, should you consider expansion by opening further outlets, and finally, this shouldn't really become a consideration until you have matured from retailer to businessman.

16

Time Management

Time management is a topic that has been written about extensively, and, in summary, tends to focus on various techniques to make the limited time that you have available more productive. My 'take' on this is not to extol the virtues of the filo-fax, PDAs, diaries, and the many other 'time-management' gadgets and systems available, but to view the problem from a different perspective, and this it not to see how you can plan your time better, but to highlight how little time you really have to do want you want to do in life – and it really is very little!

Apart from good health, the most precious commodity that you possess is time. Time is not appreciated when you are young, but as the years start to pass by, you become much more aware of its importance, especially its importance in business. If you can remember being able to park in any High Street free of charge, and you think that chart music sounds awful, you probably don't need this reminder. However, if youth is still on your side, make a mental note of the following as it will make you extremely wary of wasting time, and remove any belief that you hold about being here forever:

670,140 hours – this is the average human lifespan! If you are presently age 30, you have just 407,340 hours remaining. At the age of 40 you have only 319,740 hours, and very depressingly at the age of 50 a meagre 232,140 hours. If you work the formula backwards and deduct the age from which you would like to retire, i.e. age 65 you can deduct at least 100,000 hours from the above, if you then deduct all the holiday time that you plan to have, and the free time with family, it starts to look very bleak. Finally, even though being self-employed demands the occasional sleepless night, you must also deduct approx 30% of the remaining time (because you will most definitely need to sleep) from the figures above to establish just how much time you really have left to develop your commercial empire.

Example Age 50 (now)	**232,140 hours remaining**
Deduct	100,000 hours retiring at age 65
Deduct	? hours holiday/ family time/commuting
Deduct	? hours sleep
Deduct	? hours other
Total	?????

If you complete the above exercise, you will see how most of your life is already spoken for.

I make no apologies for repeating this but, in business, and indeed life, time is precious, and this perspective is a sobering reminder that we do indeed need to become a 'today person' and not an 'I'll do it tomorrow' person.

There are relatively few things in life that genuinely can't be done immediately, and I personally believe that leaving things until tomorrow, that could be done today, is simply down to bad habits, lack of motivation, lack of self-discipline or a combination of all three.

People are motivated to do things which are important to them. For example, you wouldn't forget to collect the keys to your new house or store on the day of legal completion, nor would you forget to visit your partner in hospital after major surgery, because these events are important to you. Equally, your business customers and staff feel that they too should command this level of commitment, because they too feel that they are important to you, and expect reciprocation. In simple terms, you should try and deal with your customers and colleagues with the same degree of motivation as you would give to your own personal important commitments. This is not about time management in a literal sense, but dedicating this level of service within a more immediate timeframe will help you to achieve what you want, when you want.

Large organisations often refer to 'meeting and exceeding customer expectations' but more often than not, only a small minority of staff actually try to do this. As an independent retailer you have no excuse.

Delaying matters until 'tomorrow' also suggests a very laid-back, and possibly slovenly approach to life. Sure, you need to prioritise, but don't fool yourself. Laziness is not a desirable trait in anybody's book. Self-discipline is probably a key factor in time management, but is seldom mentioned. It's one thing to fill a page in your diary with jobs to do, but if you lack self-discipline, chances are, the jobs won't be done. As a retailer, and possible employer, it is essential that you try extra hard to deal with all matters at the appropriate time, because you need to set an example for your employees. How else will you be able to leave your team in control if things don't get done in your presence?

Very few children understand the concept of time management, and even fewer understand the need for self-discipline, but most kids delay school homework until tomorrow in the vain hope that tomorrow will never come. However, for them, time management is a skill that can be learnt, and self-discipline will be acquired over time.

Adults have no excuse, and as a retailer and employer, you must view this subject with the enthusiasm that you hold for buying and selling stock. Try and do things on impulse, immediately – no conferring, no debating and no delaying. Do it now, not tomorrow. Earlier in the book, I mentioned the way kids naturally ask open questions, and their enthusiasm for learning and doing. It may have been a very long time since you were that young, but try and recapture some of that lost enthusiasm and keenness to do things straight away.

My view on time management is – **never waste time and always aim to action something today**. If you want to make things happen, do it now – today – not tomorrow. Of course, if you are the type of person that prefers to watch things happen, as opposed to making things happen, buy a filo-fax and plenty of post-it notes!

17

The Future

The ideas offered so far have focused on today's needs, but as today will soon be over, you need to focus on the needs of tomorrow – the future! Retailers must always plan to deal with tomorrow's customers. If you borrow money from a bank, they will certainly ask you for a copy of your three- or even five-year plan! It therefore follows that you must have an understanding about your future customers: who will they be and where will they come from?

Demographics play an essential role in marketing firms, which in turn 'feed' information to their retailer clients. Information purchased by retailers is then utilised, mainly by the chain stores and large department stores, to target new customers. Big retailers understand the need to know where their customers live, how they live, how old they are, what they buy and what they will buy in the months and years to come. Armed with this information, they can plan their strategy, their stock purchase schedules and of course, their future.

Demographics, for the uninitiated, is the scientific word used to describe population statistics. For example, where people live in the country and approximate data on local population. Their status is also determined, which would include gender, affluence and age. These are then sub-grouped into alpha-numeric codes such as B2, C3 etc, which broadly speaking place people into specific categories, such as rich, middle class, working class (white collar/blue collar workers) and so on. This data is then 'mined' by marketing groups who in turn, sell it on to the larger retailers.

Armed with this info, mail-shots and advertising media can be then directed at specific groups. I could speculate that you probably do something similar when deciding where to advertise your products, but my best guess is that you are more likely to be bullied by the local newspaper rep. to take space because it has just become available and is heavily discounted, and of course, it is the bargain of the century.

This might seem like a good idea at the time, but rarely does this type of ad hoc advertising produce any extra sales or meaningful long-term benefits.

Historians know a thing or two about the future, because they are acutely aware that history has a habit of repeating itself. Ergo, in order to understand the retailing events of the near future, we need first to look at clues from the recent past, which will point to likely events coming our way.

In the post war years (WWII), especially the 1960s, most of Europe and North America experienced a significant increase in population. Since this baby-boom period, people born in the 60s have been labelled by marketing firms as the baby boomers. A side effect of this massive increase in childbirth was the huge demand for owner-occupied property.

So, what relevance is this and what impact does this have on the future for retailers?

One legacy carried by today's mature and elderly shoppers is the guilt attached to self-indulgence. Needs generally over-rule wants, or put differently, essentials replace desirables. Baby-boomer parents were born before the Second World War and lived through very hard times. Luxury goods remained elusive to all but the most titled and therefore a spendthrift culture developed which was passed down to many of their children.

Today's kids, and many of their baby boomer parents, do not carry this legacy. They have evolved in the culture of buy now pay later. Clothes are seldom home-made or repaired but purchased or replaced with new. Cars are not just modes of transport but status symbols. This next generation of old people will not grow old gracefully, and this is evidenced, in part, by the actions of the many successful rock groups which started in the sixties and which are still performing in their sixties!

In the background, we have witnessed successive governments encouraging people to buy and own their own homes, and this is not just a recent phenomenon. As a consequence, those baby boomer parents own significant chunks of real estate. They are sitting on billions of pounds worth of what will become tomorrow's retail income.

So to answer the above question: retailers will experience consumer spending like never before. In the not to distant future, hundreds of thousands of families will start to inherit estates with values equating to a good win on the national lottery. Morbid maybe, but true.

So what will people be buying?

Many will no doubt be keen to pay off their own mortgages and debts, but these sums will pale in relation to the size of average windfalls. At the time of writing, although property values have stabilised in the USA, the UK and European property market is increasing. Modest detached homes in the South East of England now command asking prices in excess of £1 million pounds. Small-detached villas in Southern Spain, which a decade ago could be bought for around 60,000 Euros, are now being sold for 500,000 Euros. Detached villas in Florida which could be purchased for approximately $100,000 ten years ago now would set you back $250,000.

Huge sums of disposable income will be drifting around. Already, order books for large luxury yachts and boats have broken records. Second homes are being purchased, often abroad, at a frenzied pace. Does anybody wonder why Mercedes have launched a new car, called not Mercedes but Maybach? Perhaps they have already realised that too many people will soon be able to afford their top of the range S Class, and with the extremely wealthy searching for a degree of exclusivity, perhaps only a car with the price of the Maybach will allow this need to become fulfilled.

What other trends will come into play?

Well it's not by coincidence that the major cruise liner companies have commissioned new and even bigger ships to be built at the costs of tens of millions. They are intuitive enough to realise that their business will have many years of growth specifically because of this factor. And, getting back to the point – what's in this for small retailers? Well, from what I have just stated, this is the question you should be answering yourself. I can speculate, however, and suggest that anything health related, i.e. products which assist the aging and elderly will be in strong demand, especially, products and services, which help people to stay and look young. Travel Agents will become more niche and the market will adjust accordingly placing more emphasis on tailor made holidays for the over 50s. Cheap holidays will still appeal to many but short holiday breaks with quality attributes will win the day. This is assuming, of course, that all these computer literate people are not booking their holidays on-line.

With the advent of this newly acquired affluence, consider what secondary purchases will be required to allow people to fulfil their dreams. Luxury cars purchased will need lots of care and attention. Who will do this and what products will be needed for owners to give this care? Big windfalls often mean people moving to bigger houses. This in turn necessitates new furniture, carpets and so on.

Flying or cruising to exotic destinations means potential sales of new off-season clothing (hot vacations in the Winter), luggage and sun-creams. Try buying sun-related products in the UK in December!

As with most things new, we must also consider and recognise the side effects. A combination of high property values means first-time buyers are either almost excluded from property ownership and when combined with their parents' new found wealth (inheritance), they feel that the need to flee the nest is a remote necessity of the future. So, ironically, parents feel obliged to continue caring for their offspring a little while longer (on average about 10 years longer). For the 20- or 30-something child, this presents him or her with something their parents barely remember – having fun; and lots of it. Without the block and chain analogy of a mortgage, maintenance, utility bills and school fees, today's 'kids' have an extended life, which primarily revolves around clubbing, pubbing and generally having fun. So, designer clothes, gadgets, sophisticated car accessories such as sat nav, expensive skin and hair protection, and footwear will represent the equivalent of first time buyers' mortgage payments. Once again, retailers that pick up on these emerging trends and can tap into this huge pool of disposable income will be bringing home the bacon.

The over-riding message is one of future prosperity for a considerable number of people. People will have more money, and therefore more disposable income. Retailers, I believe, will be the ultimate beneficiaries. But they need to be creative and target the various niches as they evolve.

For retailers, the near future, whilst always uncertain, presents a degree of predictability. Just make sure that you are well positioned to take advantage of this opportunity when it arrives!

Trivia:

Top three most expensive retail rents in the world:

- 1st – Fifth Avenue, New York. Average rent at November 2004 is $10,226 (£5,680) per square metre

- 2nd – Champs Elysées, Paris, £4,248 per square metre. (the most expensive European Street)

- 3rd – Oxford Street, Bond Street and Brompton Road (home to Harrods), London: £3,000 per square metre

- 4th .... and you pay ... ?

Appendix

Useful UK addresses

PPL: Licensing to play sound recordings in public contact:
ppo.info@ppluk.com, Tel: 020 7534 1000, Fax: 020 7534 1111

PRS: Licensing to play sound recordings in public contact:
MCPS-PRS Alliance, Copyright House, 29-33 Berners Street, London,
W1T 3AB , Tel: 020 7580 5544

Small Business Advisory service (UK)
Small Business Service, Kingsgate House, 66-74 Victoria Street,
London, SW1E 6SW , Tel: 0845 001 0031

British Shops and Stores Association Limited
Middleton House, 2 Main Road, Middleton Cheney, Banbury, Oxon,
OX17 2TN Tel: 01295 712277 Fax: 01295 711665
email: info@bssa.co.uk web: www.british-shops.co.uk

The British Retail Consortium
BRC Trading Limited, 21 Dartmouth Street, London SW1H 9BP
Tel: +44 (0)20 7854 8984   Fax: +44 (0)20 7854 8901
Email: info@brc.co.uk Web: www.brc.org.uk

British Footwear Association
3 Burystead Place, Wellingborough, Northants, NN8 1AH
Tel: +44 (0) 1933 229005 Fax: +44 (0) 1933 225009
Email: info@britfoot.com   Web: www.britfoot,com

Association of Convenience Stores Ltd

Federation House, 7 Farnborough Street, Farnborough, Hampshire
GU14 8AG Tel: 01252 515001   Fax: 01252 515002
Web: www.thelocalshop.com

Booksellers Association of the United Kingdom & Ireland Limited

Minster House, 272 Vauxhall Bridge Road, London SW1V 1BA
Tel: 020 7802 0802. Fax: 020 7802 0803.
Email: mail@booksellers.org.uk   Web: www.booksellers.org.uk

Experian Credit reference agency UK

PO BOX 7710, Nottingham, NG80 7WE
Customer Service, Free phone: 0800 656 9000
(Mon-Fr 9am-6pm, Sat 9am-1pm) Fax: 0115 9344272
Email: CustomerService@CreditExpert.co.uk

Federation of Small Businesses,

Sir Frank Whittle Way, Blackpool Business Park, Blackpool, Lancashire
FY4 2FE
Tel: 01253 336000 Fax: 01253 348046 Web:www.fsb.org.uk

Unlike the UK, the USA tends to have very few nationwide bodies that specifically meet the needs of the small retailer. They do however, have numerous organisations that operate independently within each state, and as listing every organisation within each state would take up the equivalent space of another book, I would recommend that you list these firms by state in your favourite internet search engine. I have no doubt however, that the following list will prove useful:

National Retail Federation

325 7th Street, NW, Suite 1100, Washington, DC 20004.
Tel 202-783-7971 or Toll-free 1-800-NRF-HOW2. Fax 202-737-2849.
Web: www.nrf.com

Shop.org
325 7th Street, NW, Suite 1100, Washington, DC 20004
Tel: 202-626-8192   Fax: 202-737-2849   Web: www.shop.org

American Booksellers Association
200 White Plains Rd. Tarrytown, NY 10591
Tel: (800) 637-0037, (914) 591-2665   Fax: (914) 591-2720
Web: www.bookweb.org

Experian Credit reference agency USA
Expert Customer Care, PO Box 19729, Irvine, CA 92623-9729
Phone Call toll free: 1-866-673-0140
6am-6pm Mon thru Fri and 8am-5pm Sat and Sun (Pacific Time)
Email customerservice@creditexpert.com Postal Mail Credit

Final words from the author

Variety, they say, is the spice of life. I took this phrase too literally when I left school and could now be described as a serial careerist. Over the past twenty-odd years, I have leaped across many career paths, ranging from a short spell in the armed forces to estate agent to financial adviser to building society regional financial services manager to bank executive and presently high street retailer. After starting a retail business at the height of the early nineties recession, I can say with confidence that my wife and I have experienced most aspects of retailing the hard way. I am convinced that had the knowledge in this book been available when we first embarked on our retailing venture, we would have saved many sleepless nights, and not have been guinea pigs to so many of our suppliers and customers.

John Castell

Index

Other Management Books 2000 titles in the field of retailing

LAW FOR RETAILERS - Bill Thomas
A5 pb - 236pp - £12.99 - 2003 (new ed) - 1-85252-423-5
A practical guide for retail managers, sales people and shop assistants - anyone dealing with retail customers and suppliers. There is detailed advice on all aspects of retailers' legal obligations to customers and suppliers, and possible claims in the event of damages, breach of contract and so on.

THE RETAILER AND THE COMMUNITY - Peter Fleming with Karen McColl
A5 pb - 240pp - £12.99 - 2002 - 1-85252-219-4 I
How to raise your business profile in the community. Making your business stand out, researching your market, socially responsible retailing, getting involved and making the community work for you and advertising.

RETAIL BUYING TECHNIQUES - Fiona Elliott and Janet Rider
A5 pb - 240pp - £12.99 - 2003 - 1-85252-444-8
The acquisition of the right stock at the right price at the right time is crucial to the economic well-being of the business. This practical guide looks at planning the budget and the structure of the merchandise range, developing products and brands, sourcing, presenting and promoting.

RETAIL MANAGEMENT - Peter Fleming
A5 pb - 230pp - £12.99 - 2004 - 1-85252-464-2
An invaluable resource for all retail managers regardless of age or experience, packed with case studies, self-assessment exercises and performance tips. Leading and managing teams, setting objectives, managing stock, budgets and sales, security and safety, recruitment communications and so on.

RETAIL SELLING - EVERYONE'S BUSINESS - Peter Fleming
A5 pb - 192pp - £12.99 - 1995 - 1-85252-295-X
With more than 100 performance tips, many case histories, mini-assignments and self-test questionnaires, this book is really a complete training course in just 192 pages. Every retail salesperson should have a copy, from top managers to new shopfloor staff.

Actinic is a specialist developer of e-commerce and shopping cart software, with over 10,000 users in 40 countries worldwide. Their packages are easy to use, affordable and feature-rich, and backed up by a range of comprehensive support services and an aggressive ongoing development programme.

This free disc

This disc should operate automatically when you insert it into your computer. The instructions are clear and you should find the program easy to navigate. Good luck!